The Complete Air Fryer

COOKBOOK

On A Budget

100+ Fast and Easy Delicious Recipes for Beginners and Advanced User.
Effortless Air Frying, as Roast or Grill for Smart People

LEONARD KEY

DISCLAIMER

All Erudition contained in this book is given for informational and educational purposes only. The author is not in any way accountable for any results or outcomes that emanate from using this material. Constructive attempts have been made to provide information that is both accurate and effective, but the author is not bound for accuracy or use/misuse of information.

FOREWORD

First, I will like to thank you for taking the first step of trusting me and deciding to purchase/read this life transforming Book. Thanks for spending your time and resources on this material. I can assure you of exact blueprint I lay bare in the information manual you are currently reading. It has transformed lives, and I strongly believe it will equally transform your life too. All the information I presented in this Do-It-Yourself is easy to digest and practice.

BREAKFAST

LUNCH

SNACKS

VEGETABLE RECIPES

POULTRY

APPETIZERS

DESERTS

STREET SNACKS

BRUNCH RECIPIES

DESSERTS AND SWEETS RECIPES

TABLE OF CONTENTS

What is an air fryer?

Air fryer is a present-day kitchen appliance that cooks food by circulating hot air around it instead of using oil. It offers a light version of foods that are traditionally cooked in the fryer. As a result, mostly unhealthy foods such as French fries, fried chicken and onion rings are cooked without oil or up to 80% less fat than conventional cooking methods. An air fryer provides healthier foods and fried foods, allowing you to get rid of the calories gained by eating fried foods while providing you with a crispy texture, texture and quality. This appliance operates by circulating hot air (up to 400 ° F) evenly and quickly around food ingredients housed indoors. The heat makes the food ingredient crispy and dry on the outside but soft and moist on the inside. The fryer can be used on just about anything. In addition to frying, you can bake, bake and bake. The variety of cooking options makes it easy to prepare any type of food at any time of the day.

Why Use It

Low-Fat Meals: Unarguably, the most fundamental advantage of the air fryer is its use of hot-air course to cook food ingredients from all points, accordingly taking out the need for oil use. This makes it workable for people on low fat eating regimen to serenely get ready magnificently sound meals. More beneficial Foods& Environment: Air fryers are intended to work without stuffing oils and to deliver more advantageous foods with up to 80 percent less fat. This makes it simpler to shed pounds because you can even now eat your seared dishes while saving the calories and immersed fat. Making that change to a more advantageous life is progressively feasible by utilizing this appliance. Your house is additionally freed of the fragrance that accompanies deep singed foods that regularly remains around the climate even a few hours after deep searing.

Multipurpose Use: The air fryer empowers you to perform various tasks as it can set up numerous dishes immediately. It is your across the board appliance that can flame broil, bake, fry and meal those dishes that you love! You never again need numerous appliances for different occupations. It can do different employments separate appliances will do. It can flame broil meat, cook veggies and bake baked goods. It fills in as a compelling substitution for your broiler, deep fryer and stovetop.

Very Safe: Remember how extra cautious you must be while tossing chicken or some different ingredients into the deep fryer? You need to guarantee that the hot oil doesn't spill and consume your skin since it's in every case hot. With your airfryer, you wouldn't need to stress over brunt skin from hot oil spillage. It does all the broiling and is totally protected. By and by, use cooking gloves while repositioning your fryer to maintain a strategic distance from risks from the warmth. Moreover, keep your air fryer out of kids' span.

Simple Clean Up: The Air Fryer leaves no oil and consequently no wreckage. Clean-up time is pleasant since there oils spills to clean on dividers and floors, and no rejecting or scouring of skillet. There is no need to invest energy guaranteeing that everything is immaculate. The Air fryer parts are made of non-stick material which keeps food from adhering to surfaces, in this manner making it difficult to clean. These parts are anything but difficult to clean and keep up. They are removable and dishwasher-protected also.

Spare Valuable Time: People who are on tight timetables can utilize the quickness of the air fryer to make delightful meals. For cases, you can make French fries in under 15 minutes and bake a cake inside 25 minutes. Inside minutes as well, you can appreciate firm chicken fingers or brilliant fries. If you are consistently in a hurry, the air fryer is perfect for you because you will invest less energy in the kitchen. It empowers you to deal with your boisterous and occupied day by day life, making your day progressively sensible.

Tips For Usage

Keep It Dry: Pat dry foods before cooking, particularly marinated foods. Doing this will avert abundance smoke and splattering. Foods that contain high fat substance, for example, chicken bosom and wings typically store fat when cooking. Subsequently, make sure you void the stored fat from the base of the airfryer on occasion.

Space Your Foods: Overcrowding is a no-no with the airfryer. If you need your foods to cook well, give it a lot of space with the goal that air can course well. You need to enjoy the firmness of your meals, isn't that so? Congestion keeps air from circling over the foods. So make certain to space foods out.

Shake Foods Around: Open the Air Fryer like clockwork of cooking and shake around foods in the basket. Chips, French fries and other littler foods can pack however shaking around counteracts that. Pivot foods each 5 to 10 minutes to empower them cook and shape well.

Splash Foods: You will need your cooking splash when utilizing your airfryer as it keeps foods from adhering to the basket. Shower foods softly or you could simply include a smidgen of oil.

Cook in Batches: The airfyer has little cooking limit. If you are cooking for countless people, you should cook in batches. Preheat air fryer when it has not been used for some time.

Preheat for 3-5 minutes to permit it heat up appropriately. Presently you can use your air fryer to prepare the painstakingly chose solid and delicious plans underneath.

Essentially adhere to the guidelines and enjoy well-adjusted meals for you and your family.

SECTION ONE

Breakfast

Tomato and Bacon Breakfast

SERVING	PREP TIME	COOK TIME
6	10 MINS	13 MINS

INGREDIENTS:

1 pound of white bread, diced
1 pound of smoked bacon, cooked and chopped
¼ cup of olive oil
1 chopped yellow onion
28 ounces of canned tomatoes, chopped
½ teaspoon chopped red peppers
½ pound cheddar, shredded
2 tablespoons chives, chopped
½ pound Monterey jack, shredded
2 tablespoons stock
Salt and black pepper to the taste
8 eggs, whisked

DIRECTIONS:

1. Pour the oil to your air fryer and heat it up at 350 0 F.

2. Add your onion, tomatoes, bread, bacon, red pepper and stock and stir.

3. Then, you can add cheddar,eggs, and Monterey jack and cook everything for 20 minutes.

4. Divide among plates, sprinkle chives and you can go ahead to serve.

Enjoy!

Nutrition: fat 5, fiber 7, calories 231, carbs 12, protein 4

Delectable Hash

SERVING	PREP TIME	COOK TIME
6	10 MINS	15 MINS

INGREDIENTS:

16 ounces hash tans
¼ cup olive oil
½ teaspoon paprika
½ teaspoon garlic powder
Salt and black pepper to the taste
1 egg, whisked
2 tablespoon chives, chopped
1 cup cheddar, shredded

DIRECTIONS:

1. Pour the oil into your hot air fryer, heat it to 350 0 F and add a tan.

2. Also add pepper, garlic powder, salt, pepper and egg, mix and cook for 15 minutes.

3. Add cheddar cheese and chives, stir, arrange and serve.

Enjoy!

Nutrition: 213 calories, 7 fats, 8 fiber, 12 carbs, protein

Blackberry French Toast

SERVING	PREP TIME	COOK TIME
6	10 MINS	20 MINS

INGREDIENTS:

1 cup blackberry jam, warm
4 eggs
1 teaspoon vanilla concentrate
Cooking spray
12 ounces bread divide, cubed
1 teaspoon cinnamon powder
2 cups half and half
½ cup dim colored sugar
8 ounces cream cheddar, cubed

DIRECTIONS:

1. Grease your air fryer together with cooking spray and warmth it up at 300 0 F.

2. Add blueberry jam on the base, layer half of the strong bread shapes, by then incorporate cream cheddar and top with the rest of the bread.

3. In a bowl, blend eggs in with half and half, cinnamon, sugar and vanilla, whisk well and incorporate over bread blend.

4. Cook for 20 minutes, separate among plates and serve for breakfast. Appreciate!

Enjoy!

Nutrition: carbs 16, protein 6calories 215, fat 6, fiber 9

Smoked Sausage Breakfast Mix

SERVING	PREP TIME	COOK TIME
4	10 MINS	30 MINS

INGREDIENTS:

1 and ½ pounds smoked hotdog, chopped and sautéed A touch of salt and black pepper
1 and ½ cups corn meal
4 and ½ cups water
16 ounces cheddar, shredded
1 cup milk
¼ teaspoon garlic powder
1 and ½ teaspoons thyme, chopped
Cooking spray
4 eggs, whisked

DIRECTIONS:

1.Transfer the water in a pot, heat to the point of boiling over medium heat, add corn meal, stir, spread, cook for 5 minutes and take off heat.

2.Add cheddar, stir until it melts and mix with milk, thyme, salt, pepper, garlic powder and eggs and whisk truly well.

3.Heat up your air fryer at 300 0 F, grease with cooking spray and add carmelized wiener.

4.Add corn meal mix, spread and cook for 25 minutes.

5.Divide between meals and serve breakfast.

Enjoy!

Nutrition: 321 calories, 6 fats, 7 fiber, 17 carbs, 4 proteins

Flavorful Potato Frittata

SERVING	PREP TIME	COOK TIME
6	10 MINS	20 MINS

INGREDIENTS:

6 ounces jarred simmered red ringer peppers, chopped
12 eggs, whisked
½ cup parmesan, grated
3 garlic cloves, minced
2 tablespoons parsley, chopped
Salt and black pepper to the taste
2 tablespoons chives, chopped
16 potato wedges
6 tablespoons ricotta cheddar
Cooking spray

DIRECTIONS:

1. In a bowl, mix the eggs with red pepper, garlic, parsley, salt, pepper and ricotta and mix well.

2. Preheat the fryer to 300 0 F and apply oil spray.

3. Add half of the potato slices in half and sprinkle with half of the parmesan cheese everywhere.

4. Add half of the egg mixture, add the rest of the potatoes and the rest of the parmesan.

5. Add the rest of the egg mixture, sprinkle the chives and cook for 20 minutes.

6. Divide between meals and serve breakfast.

Enjoy!

Nutrition: 312 calories, 6 fats, 9 fiber, 16 carbs, 5 proteins

Asparagus frittata

SERVING	PREP TIME	COOK TIME
2	5 MINS	10 MINS

INGREDIENTS:

4 beaten eggs
2 tablespoons ground parmesan
4 tablespoons milk
Salt and black pepper to taste.
10 tops of asparagus, hamburger
Cooking spray

DIRECTIONS:

1. In a bowl, combine eggs with parmesan, milk, salt, and pepper and beat well.

2. Preheat the fryer to 400 ° F and oil with spray oil.

3. Add the asparagus, add the egg mixture, mix the piece and cook for 5 minutes.

4. Divide frittata between meals and serve break-fast.⊠

Enjoy!

Nutrition: calories 312, fat 5, fiber 8, carbohydrates 14, protein 2

An Amazing Breakfast Burger

MEAL	PREP TIME	COOK TIME
6	10 MINS	45 MINS

INGREDIENTS:

1 pound of beef
1 chopped yellow onion
1 teaspoon tomato puree
1 teaspoon minced garlic
1 teaspoon mustard
1 teaspoon basil, dried
1 teaspoon chopped parsley
1 tablespoon minced cheddar cheese
Salt and black pepper to taste.
4 pastries, for serving

DIRECTIONS:

1. In a bowl, mix the meat with onions, tomato puree, garlic, mustard, basil, parsley, cheese, salt and pepper, mix well and form 4 burgers with this mixture.

2. Preheat the fryer to 400 ° F, add the burgers and cook for 25 minutes.

3. Lower the temperature to 350 0 FF and cook the burgers for another 20 minutes.

4. Arrange them in pastries and serve for a quick breakfast.

Enjoy!

Nutrition: 234 calories, 5 fats, 8 fiber, 12 carbs, 4 proteins

Onion Frittata

SERVING	PREP TIME	COOK TIME
6	10 MINS	20 MINS

INGREDIENTS:

10 beaten eggs
1 tablespoon olive oil
1 pound of chopped potatoes
2 chopped yellow onions
Salt and black pepper to taste.
1 ounce grated cheddar cheese
½ cups sour cream

DIRECTIONS:

1. Into a large bowl, mix the eggs with potatoes, onions, salt, pepper, cheese and sour cream and beat well.

2. Grease the pan of your fryer with oil, add the egg mixture, place in the fryer and cook for 20 minutes at 320 2F.

3. Slice the frittata, divide between meals and serve for breakfast.⊠

Enjoy!

Nutrition: calories 11131, fat 5, fiber 7, carbohydrates 8, protein 4

Vegetables Burritos

SERVING	PREP TIME	COOK TIME
4	10 MINS	10 MINS

INGREDIENTS:

2 tablespoons kashea butter
2 tablespoons tamari
2 tablespoons water
2 tablespoons liquid smoke
4 rice paper
Alice cups of sweet potatoes, steamed and diced
½ small broccoli heads, separate flowers and 7 steamed asparagus stalks
8 roasted red peppers, chopped
A handful of chopped kale

DIRECTIONS:

1. In a bowl, combine Indian porridge butter with water, tamari and liquid smoke and mix well.

2. Moisten the rice paper and place it on the work surface.

3. Divide the sweet potatoes, broccoli, asparagus, red peppers and kale, wrap the burritos and dip them in a cashew mixture.

4. Put burritos in their deep fryer and cook at 350 0 F for 10 minutes.

5. Divide vegetarian burritos between serving plates.

Enjoy!

Nutrition: 172 calories, 4 fats, 7 fiber, 8 carbs, 3 proteins

Chicken Kabobs

SERVING	PREP TIME	COOK TIME
2	10 MINS	20 MINS

INGREDIENTS:

3 orange bell peppers, cut into squares
¼ cup honey
1/3 cup soy sauce
Salt and black pepper to the taste
Cooking spray
6 mushrooms, halved
2 chicken breasts, skinless, boneless and roughly cubed

DIRECTIONS:

1.Mix the chicken properly with pepper, salt, honey, say sauce and some cooking spray and toss well inside of a large container

2.Thread bell peppers,chicken, and mushrooms on skewers, place them in your air fryer and cook at 338 0 F for 20 minutes.

3.Divide among plates and serve for lunch.⊠

Enjoy!

Nutrition: calories 261, fat 7, fiber 9, carbs 12, protein 6

SECTION TWO

Lunch

Hamburger Lunch Meatballs

SERVING	PREP TIME	COOK TIME
4	10 MINS	15 MINS

INGREDIENTS:

½ pound meat, ground
½ pound Italian hotdog, slashed
½ teaspoon garlic powder
½ teaspoon onion powder
Salt and dark pepper to the taste
½ cup cheddar, ground
Pureed potatoes for serving

DIRECTIONS:

1.In a bowl, blend hamburger in with hotdog, garlic powder, onion powder, salt, pepper and cheddar, mix well and shape 16 meatballs out of this blend.

2.Place meatballs in your air fryer and cook them at 370 0 F for 15 minutes.

3.Serve your meatballs with some pureed potatoes as an afterthought.

Appreciate!

Nutrition: calories 333, fat 23, fiber 1, carbs 8, protein 20

Scrumptious Chicken Wings

SERVING	PREP TIME	COOK TIME
4	10 MINS	45 MINS

INGREDIENTS:

3 pounds chicken wings
½ cup margarine
1 tablespoon old straight flavoring
¾ cup potato starch
1 teaspoon lemon juice
Lemon wedges for serving

DIRECTIONS:

1.In a bowl, blend starch in with old inlet flavoring and chicken wings and hurl well.

2.Place chicken wings in your air fryer's crate and cook them at 360 0 F for 35 minutes shaking the fryer every once in a while.

3.Increase temperature to 400 0 F, cook chicken wings for 10 minutes more and gap them on plates.

4.Heat up a skillet over a delicate warmth, include spread and soften it.

5.Add lemon juice, mix well, take off warmth and sprinkle over chicken wings.

6.Serve them for lunch with lemon wedges as an afterthought.

Appreciate!

Nutrition: calories 271, fat 6, fiber 8, carbs 18, protein 18

Simple Hot Dogs

SERVING	PREP TIME	COOK TIME
2	7 MINS	10 MINS

INGREDIENTS:

2 frank buns
2 franks
1 tablespoon Dijon mustard
2 tablespoons cheddar, ground

DIRECTIONS:

1.Put franks in preheated air fryer and cook them at 390 0 F for 5 minutes.

2.Divide franks into sausage buns, spread mustard and cheddar, return everything to your air fryer and cook for 2 minutes more at 3900 F.

3.Serve for lunch.

Appreciate!

Nutrition: calories 211, fat 3, fiber 8, carbs 12, protein 4

Japanese Chicken Mix

SERVING	PREP TIME	COOK TIME
2	8 MINS	10 MINS

INGREDIENTS:

2 chicken thighs, skinless and
boneless
2 ginger cuts, slashed
3 garlic cloves, minced
¼ cup soy sauce
¼ cup mirin
1/8 cup purpose
½ teaspoon sesame oil
08059800209
1/8 cup water
2 tablespoons sugar
1 tablespoon of cornstarch
blended in with two tablespoons
water Sesame seeds for serving

DIRECTIONS:

1.In a bowl, blend chicken thighs in with ginger, garlic, soy sauce, mirin, purpose, oil, water, sugar and cornstarch, hurl well, move to preheated air fryer and cook at 360 0 F for 8 minutes.

2.Divide among plates, sprinkle sesame seeds on top and present with a side serving of mixed greens for lunch.

Appreciate!

Nutrition: calories 300, fat 7, fiber 9, carbs 17, protein 10

Lentils Fritters

SERVING	PREP TIME	COOK TIME
2	10 MINS	10 MINS

INGREDIENTS:

1 cup yellow lentils, absorbed water for 1 hour and depleted
1 hot stew pepper, slashed
1 inch ginger piece, ground
½ teaspoon turmeric powder
1 teaspoon garam masala
1 teaspoon preparing powder
Salt and dark pepper to the taste
2 teaspoons olive oil
1/3 cup water
½ cup cilantro, hacked
1 and ½ cup spinach, hacked
4 garlic cloves, minced
¾ cup red onion, hacked
Mint chutney for serving

DIRECTIONS:

1.In your blender, blend lentils in with bean stew pepper, ginger, turmeric, garam masala, heating powder, salt, pepper, olive oil, water, cilantro, spinach, onion and garlic, mix well and shape medium balls out of this blend.

2.Place them all in your preheated air fryer at 400F and cook for 10 minutes.

3.Serve your veggie wastes with a side plate of mixed greens for lunch.

Appreciate!

Nutrition: calories 142, fat 2, fiber 8, carbs 12, protein

Creamy Chicken Stew

SERVING	PREP TIME	COOK TIME
4	10 MINS	25 MINS

INGREDIENTS:

1 and ½ cups canned cream of celery soup
6 chicken tenders
Salt and black pepper to the taste
2 potatoes, chopped
1 bay leaf
1 thyme spring, chopped
1 tablespoon milk
1 egg yolk
½ cup heavy cream

DIRECTIONS:

1.In a bowl, mix chicken with cream of celery, potatoes, heavy cream, bay leaf, thyme, salt and pepper, toss, pour into your air fryer's pan and cook at 320 0 F for 25 minutes.

2.Leave your stew to cool down a bit, discard bay leaf, divide among plates and serve right away.

Enjoy!

Nutrition: calories 300, fat 11, fiber 2, carbs 23, protein 14

Lunch
Pork and Potatoes

SERVING	PREP TIME	COOK TIME
2	10 MINS	25 MINS

INGREDIENTS:

2 pounds pork loin
Salt and black pepper to the taste
2 red potatoes, cut into medium wedges
½ teaspoon garlic powder
½ teaspoon red pepper flakes
1 teaspoon parsley, dried
A drizzle of balsamic vinegar

DIRECTIONS:

1.In your air fryer's pan, mix pork with potatoes, salt, pepper, garlic powder, pepper flakes, parsley and vinegar, toss and cook at 390 0 F for 25 minutes.

2.Slice pork, divide it and potatoes on plates and serve for lunch.

Enjoy!

Nutrition: calories 400, fat 15, fiber 7, carbs 27, protein 20

Easy Chicken Lunch

SERVING	PREP TIME	COOK TIME
6	10 MINS	20 MINS

INGREDIENTS:

1 bunch kale, chopped
Salt and black pepper to the taste
¼ cup chicken stock
1 cup chicken, shredded
3 carrots, chopped
1 cup shiitake mushrooms, roughly sliced

DIRECTIONS:

1.In a blender, mix stock with kale, pulse a few times and pour into a pan that fits your air fryer.

2.Add salt,mushrooms, carrots, chicken, and pepper to the taste, toss, introduce in your air fryer and cook at 350 0 F for 18 minutes.

Enjoy!

Nutrition: calories 180, fat 7, fiber 2, carbs 10, protein 5

Corn with Lime and Cheese

SERVING	PREP TIME	COOK TIME
2	10 MINS	15 MINS

INGREDIENTS:

2 corns on the cob, husks removed
A drizzle of olive oil
½ cup feta cheese, grated
2 teaspoons sweet paprika
Juice from 2 limes

DIRECTIONS:

1.Rub corn with oil and paprika, place in your air fryer and cook at 400 0 F for 15 minutes, flipping once.

2.Divide corn on plates, sprinkle cheese on top, drizzle lime juice and serve as a side dish.

Enjoy!

Nutrition: calories 200, fat 5, fiber 2, carbs 6, protein 6

Fried Tomatoes

SERVING	PREP TIME	COOK TIME
4	5 MINS	10 MINS

INGREDIENTS:

2 green tomatoes, sliced
Salt and black pepper to the taste
½ cup flour
1 cup buttermilk
1 cup panko bread crumbs
½ tablespoon Creole seasoning
Cooking spray

DIRECTIONS:

1. Season tomato slices with salt and pepper.

2. Put flour in a bowl, buttermilk in another and panko crumbs and Creole seasoning in a third one

3. Dredge tomato slices in flour, then in buttermilk and panko bread crumbs, place them in your air fryer's basket greased with cooking spray and cook them at 400 0 F for 5 minutes

4. Share among plates and serve as a side dish.

Enjoy!

Nutrition: calories 124, fat 5, fiber 7, carbs 9, protein 4

Vermouth Mushrooms

SERVING	PREP TIME	COOK TIME
4	10 MINS	25 MINS

INGREDIENTS:

1 tablespoon olive oil
2 pounds white mushrooms
2 tablespoons white vermouth
2 teaspoons herbs de Provence
2 garlic cloves, minced

DIRECTIONS:

11.In your air fryer, mix oil with mushrooms, herbs de Provence and garlic, toss and cook at 350 0 F for 20 minutes.

2.Add vermouth, toss and cook for 5 minutes more.

3.Share among plates and serve as a side dish.

Enjoy!

Nutrition: calories 121, fat 2, fiber 5, carbs 7, protein 4

Roasted Parsnips

SERVING	PREP TIME	COOK TIME
6	10 MINS	40 MINS

INGREDIENTS:

2 pounds parsnips, peeled and cut into medium chunks
2 tablespoons maple syrup
1 tablespoon parsley flakes, dried
1 tablespoon olive oil

DIRECTIONS:

1.Preheat your air fryer at 360 0 F, add oil and heat it up as well.

2.Add parsnips, maple syrup, and parsley flakes toss and cook them for 40 minutes

3.Share among plates and serve as a side dish.

Enjoy!

Nutrition: calories 124, fat 3, fiber 3, carbs 7, protein 4

SECTION THREE

Snacks

Tortilla Chips

SERVING	PREP TIME	COOK TIME
4	6 MINS	10 MINS

INGREDIENTS:

8 corn tortillas, cut into triangles
Salt and black pepper to the
taste
1 tablespoon olive oil
A pinch of garlic powder
A pinch of sweet paprika

DIRECTIONS:

1.In a bowl, mix tortilla chips with oil, add salt, pepper, garlic powder and paprika, toss well, place them in your air fryer's basket and cook them at 400 0 F for 6 minutes.

2.Serve them as a side for a fish dish.⊠

Enjoy!

Nutrition: calories 53, fat 1, fiber 1, carbs 6, protein 4

Zucchini Croquettes

SERVING	PREP TIME	COOK TIME
4	10 MINS	10 MINS

INGREDIENTS:

1 carrot, grated
1 zucchini, grated
2 slices of bread, crumbled
1 egg
Salt and black pepper to the taste
½ teaspoon sweet paprika
1 teaspoon garlic, minced
2 tablespoons parmesan cheese, grated
1 tablespoon corn flour

DIRECTIONS:

1.Put zucchini in a bowl, add salt, leave aside for 10 minutes, squeeze excess water and transfer them to another bowl.

2.Add carrots, salt, pepper, paprika, garlic, flour, parmesan, egg and bread crumbs, stir well, shape 8 croquettes, place them in your air fryer and cook at 360 0 F for about 10 minutes

3.Share among plates and serve as a side dish

Enjoy it!

Nutrition: calories 102, fat 3, fiber 2, carbs 7, protein 4

Creamy Potatoes

SERVING	PREP TIME	COOK TIME
4	10 MINS	20 MINS

INGREDIENTS:

1 a ½ pounds potatoes, peeled and cubed
2 tablespoons olive oil
Salt and black pepper to the taste
1 tablespoon hot paprika
1 cup Greek yogurt

DIRECTIONS:

1.Put potatoes in a bowl, add water to cover, leave aside for 10 minutes, drain, pat dry them, transfer to another bowl, add salt, pepper, paprika and half of the oil and toss them well.

2.Put potatoes in your air fryer's basket and cook at 360 0 F for 20 minutes.

3.In a bowl, mix yogurt with salt, pepper and the rest of the oil and whisk.

4.Divide potatoes on plates, drizzle yogurt dressing all over, toss them and serve as a side dish.

Enjoy!

Nutrition: calories 170, fat 3, fiber 5, carbs 20, protein 5

Mexican Apple Snack

SERVING	PREP TIME	COOK TIME
4	5 MINS	10 MINS

INGREDIENTS:

3 big apples, cored, peeled and cubed
2 teaspoons lemon juice
¼ cup pecans, chopped
½ cup dark chocolate chips
½ cup clean caramel sauce

DIRECTIONS:

1.In a bowl, mix apples with lemon juice, stir and transfer to a pan that fits your air fryer.

2.Add chocolate chips, pecans, drizzle the caramel sauce, toss, introduce in your air fryer and cook at 320 0 F for 5 minutes.

3.Toss gently, divide into small bowls and serve right away as a snack.

Enjoy the Meal!

Nutrition: fat 4, fiber 3, calories 200, carbs 20, protein 3

Shrimp Muffins

SERVING	PREP TIME	COOK TIME
6	10 MINS	26 MINS

INGREDIENTS:

1 spaghetti squash, peeled and halved
2 tablespoons mayonnaise
1 cup mozzarella, shredded
8 ounces shrimp, peeled, cooked and chopped
1 and ½ cups panko
1 teaspoon parsley flakes
1 garlic clove, minced
Salt and black pepper to the taste
Cooking spray

DIRECTIONS:

1.Put squash halves in your air fryer, cook at 350 0 F for 16 minutes, leave aside to cool down and scrape flesh into a bowl.

2.Add salt, pepper, parsley flakes, panko, shrimp, mayo and mozzarella and stir well.

3.Spray a muffin tray that fits your air fryer with cooking spray and divide squash and shrimp mix in each cup.

4.Introduce in the fryer and cook at 360 0 F for 10 minutes.

5.Arrange muffins on a platter and serve as a snack.

Enjoy!

Nutrition: calories 60, fat 2, fiber 0.4, carbs 4, protein 4

Zucchini Cakes

SERVING	PREP TIME	COOK TIME
12	10 MINS	12 MINS

INGREDIENTS:

Cooking spray
½ cup dill, chopped
1 egg
½ cup whole wheat flour
Salt and black pepper to the taste
1 yellow onion, chopped
2 garlic cloves, minced
3 zucchinis, grated

DIRECTIONS:

1.In a bowl, mix zucchinis with garlic, onion, flour, salt, pepper, egg and dill, stir well, shape small patties out of this mix, spray them with cooking spray, place them in your air fryer's basket and cook at 370 0 F for 6 minutes on each side.

2.Serve them as a snack right away.

Enjoy!

Nutrition: calories 60, fat 1, fiber 2, carbs 6, protein 2

Cauliflower Bars

SERVING	PREP TIME	COOK TIME
12	10 MINS	25 MINS

INGREDIENTS:

1 big cauliflower head, florets separated
½ cup mozzarella, shredded
¼ cup egg whites
1 teaspoon Italian seasoning
Salt and black pepper to the taste

DIRECTIONS:

1.Put cauliflower florets in your food processor, pulse well, spread on a lined baking sheet that fits your air fryer, introduce in the fryer and cook at 360 0 F for 10 minutes.

2.Transfer cauliflower to a bowl, add salt, pepper, cheese, egg whites and Italian seasoning, stir really well, spread this into a rectangle pan that fits your air fryer, press well, introduce in the fryer and cook at 360 0 F for 15 minutes more.

3.Cut into 12 bars, arrange them on a platter and serve as a snack

Enjoy!

Nutrition: calories 50, fat 1, fiber 2, carbs 3, protein 3

Crispy Radish Chips

SERVING	PREP TIME	COOK TIME
4	10 MINS	10 MINS

INGREDIENTS:

Cooking spray
15 radishes, sliced
Salt and black pepper to the taste
1 tablespoon chives, chopped

DIRECTIONS:

1.Arrange radish slices in your air fryer's basket, spray them with cooking oil, season with salt and black pepper to the taste, cook them at 350 0 F for 10 minutes, flipping them halfway, transfer to bowls and serve with chives sprinkled on top.

Enjoy!

Nutrition: calories 80, fat 1, fiber 1, carbs 1, protein 1

Chickpeas Snack

SERVING	PREP TIME	COOK TIME
4	10 MINS	10 MINS

INGREDIENTS:

15 ounces canned chickpeas, drained
½ teaspoon cumin, ground
1 tablespoon olive oil
1 teaspoon smoked paprika
Salt and black pepper to the taste

DIRECTIONS:

1.In a bowl, mix chickpeas with oil, cumin, paprika, salt and pepper, toss to coat, place them in your fryer's basket and cook at 390 0 F for 10 minutes.
2.Separate into bowls and you can serve as a snack.

Enjoy!

Nutrition: fiber 6, carbs 20, calories 140, fat 1, protein 6

SECTION FOUR

Seafood Recipes

Crispy Shrimp

SERVING	PREP TIME	COOK TIME
4	10 MINS	5 MINS

INGREDIENTS:

12 big shrimp, deveined and peeled
2 egg whites
1 cup coconut, shredded
1 cup panko bread crumbs
1 cup white flour
Salt and black pepper to the taste

DIRECTIONS:

1.In a bowl, mix panko with coconut and stir.

2.Put flour, pepper and salt in a second bowl and whisk egg whites in a third one.

3.Dip shrimp in flour, egg whites mix and coconut, place them all in your air fryer's basket, cook at 350 0 F for 10 minutes flipping halfway.

4.Set out on a platter and serve as an appetizer.

Enjoy!

Nutrition: calories 140, fat 4, fiber 0, carbs 3, protein 4

Cajun Shrimp Appetizer

SERVING	PREP TIME	COOK TIME
2	10 MINS	5 MINS

INGREDIENTS:

20 tiger shrimp, peeled and deveined
Salt and black pepper to the taste
½ teaspoon old bay seasoning
1 tablespoon olive oil
¼ teaspoon smoked paprika

DIRECTIONS:

1.In a bowl, mix shrimp with oil, salt, pepper, old bay seasoning and paprika and toss to coat.

2.Place shrimp in your air fryer's basket and cook at 390 0 F for 5 minutes.

3.Set them out on a platter & serve as an appetizer.

Enjoy!

Nutrition: calories 162, fat 6, fiber 4, carbs 8, protein 14

Crispy Fish Sticks

SERVING	PREP TIME	COOK TIME
2	10 MINS	12 MINS

INGREDIENTS:

4 ounces bread crumbs
4 tablespoons olive oil
1 egg, whisked
4 white fish filets, boneless, skinless and cut into medium sticks Salt and black pepper to the taste

DIRECTIONS:

1.In a bowl, mix bread crumbs with oil and stir well.

2.Put egg in a second bowl, add salt and pepper and whisk well.

3.Dip fish stick in egg and them in bread crumb mix, place them in your air fryer's basket and cook at 360 0 F for 12 minutes.

4.Set out fish sticks on a platter and serve as an appetizer.

Enjoy!

Nutrition: calories 160, fat 3, fiber 5, carbs 12, protein 3

Shrimp and Chestnut Rolls

SERVING	PREP TIME	COOK TIME
4	10 MINS	15 MINS

INGREDIENTS:

½ pound already cooked shrimp, chopped 8 ounces water chestnuts, chopped
½ pounds shiitake mushrooms, chopped
2 cups cabbage, chopped
2 tablespoons olive oil
1 garlic clove, minced
1 teaspoon ginger, grated
3 scallions, chopped
Salt and black pepper to the taste
1 tablespoon water
1 egg yolk
6 spring roll wrappers

DIRECTIONS:

1.Heat the oil in a pan over medium high heat, add cabbage, shrimp, chestnuts, mushrooms, garlic, ginger, scallions, salt and pepper, stir and cook for 2 minutes.

2.In a bowl, mix egg with water and stir well.

3.Arrange roll wrappers on a working surface, divide shrimp and veggie mix on them, seal edges with egg wash, place them all in your air fryer's basket, cook at 360 0 F for 15 minutes, transfer to a platter and serve as an appetizer.

Enjoy!

Nutrition: calories 140, fat 3, fiber 1, carbs 12, protein 3

Seafood Appetizer

SERVING	PREP TIME	COOK TIME
4	10 MINS	25 MINS

INGREDIENTS:

½ cup yellow onion, chopped
1 cup green bell pepper, chopped
1 cup celery, chopped
1 cup baby shrimp, peeled and deveined
1 cup crabmeat, flaked
1 cup homemade mayonnaise
1 teaspoon Worcestershire sauce
Salt and black pepper to the taste
2 tablespoons bread crumbs
1 tablespoon butter
1 teaspoon sweet paprika

DIRECTIONS:

1.In a bowl, mix shrimp with crab meat, bell pepper, onion, mayo, celery, salt and pepper and stir.

2.Add Worcestershire sauce, stir again and pour everything into a baking dish that fits your air fryer.

3.Sprinkle bread crumbs and add butter, introduce in your air fryer and cook at 320 0 F for 25 minutes, shaking halfway.

4.Divide into bowl and serve with paprika sprinkled on top as an appetizer.

Enjoy!

Nutrition: calories 200, fat 1, fiber 2, carbs 5, protein 1

SECTION FIVE

Beef Recipes

Salmon Meatballs

SERVING	PREP TIME	COOK TIME
4	10 MINS	12 MINS

INGREDIENTS:

Cilantro, minced (3 Teaspoons)
1 small yellow onion, chopped
1 egg white
1 pound salmon, skinless and chopped
Black pepper and salt
2 minced garlic cloves
½ Teaspoonful of paprika
¼ cup panko
½ teaspoon oregano, ground
Cooking spray

DIRECTIONS:

1.In your food processor, mix salmon with onion, cilantro, egg white, garlic cloves, salt, pepper, paprika and oregano and stir well.

2.Add panko, blend again and shape meatballs from this mix making use of your palms,

3.Set them in thebasket of yourair fryer and spray them with cooking spray and cook at 320 0 F for 12 minutes shaking the fryer halfway.

4.Arrange meatballs on a platter and serve them as an appetizer.

Enjoy!

Nutrition: calories 289, fat 12, fiber 3, carbs 22, protein 23

Easy Chicken Wings

SERVING	PREP TIME	COOK TIME
2	10 MINS	1 HOUR

INGREDIENTS:

16 pieces chicken wings
Salt and black pepper to the taste
¼ cup butter
¾ cup potato starch
¼ cup honey
4 tablespoons garlic, minced

DIRECTIONS:

1.In a bowl, mix chicken wings with salt, pepper and potato starch, toss well, transfer to your air fryer's basket, cook them at 380 0 F for 25 minutes and at 400 0 F for 5 minutes more.

2.Meanwhile, heat up a pan with the butter over medium high heat, melt it, add garlic, stir, cook for 5 minutes and then mix with salt, pepper and honey.

3.Whisk well, cook over medium heat for 20 minutes and take off heat.

4.Arrange chicken wings on a platter, drizzle honey sauce all over and serve as an appetizer.

Enjoy!

Nutrition: calories 244, fat 7, fiber 3, carbs 19, protein 8

Chicken Breast Rolls

SERVING	PREP TIME	COOK TIME
4	10 MINS	22 MINS

INGREDIENTS:

2 cups baby spinach
4 chicken breasts, boneless and skinless
1 cup sun dried tomatoes, chopped
Salt and black pepper to the taste
1 and ½ tablespoons Italian seasoning
4 mozzarella slices
A drizzle of olive oil

DIRECTIONS:

1.Flatten chicken breasts using a meat tenderizer, divide tomatoes, mozzarella and spinach, season with salt, pepper and Italian seasoning, roll and seal them.

2.Place them in your air fryer's basket, drizzle some oil over them and cook at 375 0 F for 17 minutes, flipping once.

3.Arrange chicken rolls on a platter and serve them as an appetizer.

Enjoy!

Nutrition: calories 300, fat 1, fiber 4, carbs 7, protein 10

Crispy Chicken Breast Sticks

SERVING	PREP TIME	COOK TIME
4	10 MINS	16 MINS

INGREDIENTS:

¾ cup white flour
1 pound chicken breast, skinless, boneless and cut into medium sticks
1 teaspoon sweet paprika
1 cup panko bread crumbs
1 egg, whisked
Salt and black pepper to the taste
½ tablespoon olive oil
Zest from 1 lemon, grated

DIRECTIONS:

1.In a bowl, mix paprika with flour, salt, pepper and lemon zest and stir.

2.Put whisked egg in another bowl and the panko breadcrumbs in a third one.

3.Dredge chicken pieces in flour, egg and panko and place them in your lined air fryer's basket, drizzle the oil over them, cook at 400 0 F for 8 minutes, flip and cook for 8 more minutes.

4.Set them on a platter and serve as a snack.

Enjoy!

Nutrition: calories 254, fat 4, fiber 7, carbs 20, protein 22

Beef Rolls

SERVING	PREP TIME	COOK TIME
4	10 MINS	14 MINS

INGREDIENTS:

2 pounds beef steak, opened and flattened with a meat tenderizer Salt and black pepper to the taste
1 cup baby spinach
3 ounces red bell pepper, roasted and chopped
6 slices provolone cheese
3 tablespoons pesto

DIRECTIONS:

1.Arrange flattened beef steak on a cutting board, spread pesto all over, add cheese in a single layer, add bell peppers, spinach, salt and pepper to the taste.

2.Roll your steak, secure with toothpicks, season again with salt and pepper, place roll in your air fryer's basket and cook at 400 0 F for 14 minutes, rotating roll halfway.

3.Leave aside to cool down, cut into 2 inch smaller rolls, arrange on a platter and serve them as an appetizer.

Enjoy!

Nutrition: calories 230, fat 1, fiber 3, carbs 12, protein 10

Empanadas

SERVING	PREP TIME	COOK TIME
4	10 MINS	25 MINS

INGREDIENTS:

1 package empanada shells
1 tablespoon olive oil
1 pound beef meat, ground
1 yellow onion, chopped
Salt and black pepper to the taste
2 garlic cloves, minced
½ teaspoon cumin, ground
¼ cup tomato salsa
1 whisked egg yolk with 1 tablespoon water
1 chopped green bell pepper

DIRECTIONS:

1. up the oil in a pan over medium high heat, add beef and brown on all sides.

2. Add onion, garlic, salt, pepper, bell pepper and tomato salsa, stir and cook for 15 minutes.

3. Divide cooked meat in empanada shells, brush them with egg wash and seal.

4. Place them in your air fryer's steamer basket and cook at 350 0 F for 10 minutes.

5. Set them on a platter and serve as an appetizer.

Enjoy!

Nutrition: calories 274, fat 17, fiber 14, carbs 20, protein 7

Greek Lamb Meatballs

SERVING	PREP TIME	COOK TIME
10	10 MINS	8 MINS

INGREDIENTS:

Lamb meat, minced (4 ounces)
Black pepper and salt
A slice of bread, toasted and crumbled
2 crumbled tablespoons feta cheese
½ Tablespoon lemon peel, grated
1 tablespoon oregano, chopped

DIRECTIONS:

1.In a bowl, combine meat with bread crumbs, salt, pepper, feta, oregano and lemon peel, stir well, shape 10 meatballs and arrange them neatly

2.At 400 0 F, cook for 8 minutes, arrange them on a platter and serve as an appetizer.

Enjoy!

Nutrition: calories 234, fat 12, fiber 2, carbs 20, protein 30

Beef Party Rolls

SERVING	PREP TIME	COOK TIME
4	10 MINS	15 MINS

INGREDIENTS:

14 ounces beef stock
7 ounces white wine
4 beef cutlets
Salt and black pepper to the taste
8 sage leaves
4 ham slices
1 tablespoon butter, melted

DIRECTIONS:

1.Heat up a pan with the stock over medium high heat, add wine, cook until it reduces, take off heat and divide into small bowls

2.Season cutlets with salt and pepper, cover with sage and roll each in ham slices.

3.Brush rolls with butter, place them in your air fryer's basket and cook at 400 0 F for 15 minutes.

4.Arrange rolls on a platter and serve them with the gravy on the side.

Enjoy!

Nutrition: calories 260, fat 12, fiber 1, carbs 22, protein 21

Herbed Tomatoes Appetizer

SERVING	PREP TIME	COOK TIME
2	10 MINS	20 MINS

INGREDIENTS:

2 tomatoes, halved
Cooking spray
Salt and black pepper to the taste
1 teaspoon parsley, dried
1 teaspoon basil, dried
1 teaspoon oregano, dried
1 teaspoon rosemary, dried

DIRECTIONS:

1.Spray tomato halves with cooking oil, season with salt, pepper, parsley, basil, oregano and rosemary over them.

2.Place them in your air fryer's basket and cook at 320 0 F for 20 minutes.

3.Set them on a platter and serve as an appetizer.⊠

Enjoy!

Nutrition: calories 100, fat 1, fiber 1, carbs 4, protein 1

Olives Balls

SERVING	PREP TIME	COOK TIME
6	10 MINS	4 MINS

INGREDIENTS:

8 black olives, pitted and minced
Salt and black pepper to the taste
2 tablespoons sun dried tomato pesto
14 pepperoni slices, chopped
4 ounces cream cheese
1 tablespoons basil, chopped

DIRECTIONS:

1.In a bowl, mix cream cheese with salt, pepper, basil, pepperoni, pesto and black olives, stir well and shape small balls out of this mix.

2.Place them in your air fryer's basket, cook at 350 0 F for 4 minutes, arrange on a platter and serve as a snack.

Enjoy!

Nutrition: calories 100, fat 1, fiber 0, carbs 8, protein 3

Jalapeno Balls

SERVING	PREP TIME	COOK TIME
3	10 MINS	4 MINS

INGREDIENTS:

3 bacon slices, cooked and crumbled
3 ounces cream cheese
¼ teaspoon onion powder
Salt and black pepper to the taste
1 jalapeno pepper, chopped
½ teaspoon parsley, dried
¼ teaspoon garlic powder

DIRECTIONS:

1.In a bowl, mix cream cheese with jalapeno pepper, onion and garlic powder, parsley, bacon salt and pepper and stir well.

2.Shape small balls out of this mix, place them in your air fryer's basket, cook at 350 0 F for 4 minutes, arrange on a platter and serve as an appetizer.

Enjoy!

Nutrition: calories 172, fat 4, fiber 1, carbs 12, protein 5

Wrapped Shrimp

SERVING	PREP TIME	COOK TIME
16	10 MINS	8 MINS

INGREDIENTS:

2 tablespoons olive oil
10 ounces already cooked
shrimp, peeled and deveined
1 tablespoons mint, chopped
1/3 cup blackberries, ground
11 prosciutto sliced
1/3 cup red wine

DIRECTIONS:

1.Wrap each shrimp in a prosciutto slices, drizzle the oil over them, rub well, place in your preheated air fryer at 3900F and fry them for 8 minutes.

2.Meanwhile, heat up a pan with ground blackberries over medium heat, add mint and wine, stir, cook for 3 minutes and take off heat.

3.Set the shrimp on a platter, drizzle blackberries sauce over them and serve as an appetizer.

Enjoy!

Nutrition: calories 224, fat 12, fiber 2, carbs 12, protein 14

Broccoli Patties

SERVING	PREP TIME	COOK TIME
12	10 MINS	10 MINS

INGREDIENTS:

4 cups broccoli florets
1 and ½ cup almond flour
1 teaspoon paprika
Salt and black pepper to the taste
2 eggs
¼ cup olive oil
2 cups cheddar cheese, grated
1 teaspoon garlic powder
½ teaspoon apple cider vinegar
½ teaspoon baking soda

DIRECTIONS:

1.Set the broccoli florets in your food processor, add salt and pepper, blend well and transfer to a bowl.

2.Add almond flour, salt, pepper, paprika, garlic powder, baking soda, cheese, oil, eggs and vinegar, stir well and shape 12 patties out of this mix.

3.Place them in your preheated air fryer's basket and cook at 350 0 F for 10 minutes.

4.Arrange patties on a platter and serve as an appetizer.

Enjoy!

Nutrition: calories 203, fat 12, fiber 2, carbs 14, protein 2

Different Stuffed Peppers

SERVING	PREP TIME	COOK TIME
6	10 MINS	20 MINS

INGREDIENTS:

1 pound mini bell peppers, halved
Salt and black pepper to the taste
1 teaspoon garlic powder
1 teaspoon sweet paprika
½ teaspoon oregano, dried
¼ teaspoon red pepper flakes
1 pound beef meat, ground
1 and ½ cups cheddar cheese, shredded
1 tablespoons chili powder
1 teaspoon cumin, ground
Sour cream for serving

DIRECTIONS:

1.In a bowl, mix chili powder with paprika, salt, pepper, cumin, oregano, pepper flakes and garlic powder and stir.

2.Over medium heat,heat up your pan add beef, stir and brown for 10 minutes.

3.Add chili powder mix, stir, take off heat and stuff pepper halves with this mix.

4.Sprinkle cheese all over, place peppers in your air fryer's basket and cook them at 350 0 F for 6 minutes.

5.Arrange peppers on a platter and serve them with sour cream on the side.

Enjoy!

Nutrition: calories 170, fat 22, fiber 3, carbs 6, protein 27

Cheesy Zucchini Snack

SERVING	PREP TIME	COOK TIME
4	10 MINS	8 MINS

INGREDIENTS:

1 cup mozzarella, shredded
¼ cup tomato sauce
1 zucchini, sliced
Salt and black pepper to the taste
A pinch of cumin
Cooking spray

DIRECTIONS:

1.Arrange zucchini slices in your air fryer's basket, spray them with cooking oil, spread tomato sauce all over, them, season with salt, pepper, cumin, sprinkle mozzarella at the end and cook them at 320 0 F for 8 minutes.

2.Set them on a platter and serve as a snack.

Enjoy!

Nutrition: calories 150, fat 4, fiber 2, carbs 12, protein 4

Tasty Air Fried Cod

PREP TIME	COOK TIME
10 MINS	12 MINS

INGREDIENTS:

2 cod fish, 7 ounces each
A drizzle of sesame oil
Salt and black pepper to the
taste
1 cup water
1 teaspoon dark soy sauce
4 tablespoons light soy sauce
1 tablespoon sugar
3 tablespoons olive oil
4 ginger slices
3 spring onions, chopped
2 tablespoons coriander,
chopped

DIRECTIONS:

1.Season fish with salt, pepper, drizzle sesame oil, rub well and leave aside for 10 minutes.

2.Add fish to your air fryer and cook at 356 0 F for 12 minutes.

3.Meanwhile, heat up a pot with the water over medium heat, add dark and light soy sauce and sugar, stir, bring to a simmer and take off heat.

4.Heat up a pan with the olive oil over medium heat, add ginger and green onions, stir, cook for a few minutes and take off heat.

5.Divide fish on plates, top with ginger and green onions, drizzle soy sauce mix, sprinkle coriander and serve right away.

Enjoy!

Nutrition: calories 300, fat 17, fiber 8, carbs 20, protein 22

Buttered Shrimp Skewers

SERVING	PREP TIME	COOK TIME
2	10 MINS	6 MINS

INGREDIENTS:

8 shrimps, peeled and deveined
4 garlic cloves, minced
Salt and black pepper to the taste
8 green bell pepper slices
1 tablespoon rosemary, chopped
1 tablespoon butter, melted

DIRECTIONS:

1.In a bowl, mix shrimp with garlic, butter, salt, pepper, rosemary and bell pepper slices, toss to coat and leave aside for 10 minutes.

2.Arrange 2 shrimp and 2 bell pepper slices on a skewer and repeat with the rest of the shrimp and bell pepper pieces.

3.Place them all in your air fryer's basket and cook at 360 0 F for 6 minutes.

4.Divide among plates and serve right away.

Enjoy!

Nutrition: calories 140, fat 1, fiber 12, carbs 15, protein 7

Asian Salmon

SERVING	PREP TIME	COOK TIME
2	1 HOUR	15 MINS

INGREDIENTS:

2 medium salmon fillets
6 tablespoons light soy sauce
3 teaspoons mirin
1 teaspoon water
6 tablespoons honey

DIRECTIONS:

1.In a bowl, mix soy sauce with honey, water and mirin, whisk well, add salmon, rub well and leave aside in the fridge for 1 hour.

2.Transfer salmon to your air fryer and cook at 360 0 F for 15 minutes, flipping them after 7 minutes.

3.Meanwhile, put the soy marinade in a pan, heat up over medium heat, whisk well, cook for 2 minutes and take off heat.

4.Divide salmon on plates, drizzle marinade all over and serve.

Enjoy!

Nutrition: calories 300, fat 12, fiber 8, carbs 13, protein 24

Cod Steaks with Plum Sauce

SERVING	PREP TIME	COOK TIME
2	10 MINS	20 MINS

INGREDIENTS:

2 big cod steaks
Salt and black pepper to the taste
½ teaspoon garlic powder
½ teaspoon ginger powder
¼ teaspoon turmeric powder
1 tablespoon plum sauce
Cooking spray

DIRECTIONS:

1.Season cod steaks with salt and pepper, spray them with cooking oil, add garlic powder, ginger powder and turmeric powder and rub well.

2.Place cod steaks in your air fryer and cook at 360 0 F for 15 minutes, flipping them after 7 minutes.

3.Heat up a pan over medium heat, add plum sauce, stir and cook for 2 minutes.

4.Divide cod steaks on plates, drizzle plum sauce all over and serve.

Enjoy!

Nutrition: calories 250, fat 7, fiber 1, carbs 14, protein 12

Salmon with Capers and Mash

SERVING	PREP TIME	COOK TIME
4	10 MINS	20 MINS

INGREDIENTS:

4 salmon fillets, skinless and boneless
1 tablespoon capers, drained
Salt and black pepper to the taste
Juice from 1 lemon
2 teaspoons olive oil
For the potato mash:
2 tablespoons olive oil
1 tablespoon dill, dried
1 pound potatoes, chopped
½ cup milk

DIRECTIONS:

1.Put potatoes in a pot, add water to cover, add some salt, bring to a boil over medium high heat, cook for 15 minutes, drain, transfer to a bowl, mash with a potato masher, add 2 tablespoons oil, dill, salt, pepper and milk, whisk well and leave aside for now.

2.Season salmon with salt and pepper, drizzle 2 teaspoons oil over them, rub, transfer to your air fryer's basket, add capers on top, cook at 360 0 F and cook for 8 minutes.

3.Divide salmon and capers on plates, add mashed potatoes on the side, drizzle lemon juice all over and serve.

Enjoy!

Nutrition: calories 300, fat 17, fiber 8, carbs 12, protein 18

Asian Halibut

SERVING	PREP TIME	COOK TIME
3	30 MINS	10 MINS

INGREDIENTS:

1 pound halibut steaks
2/3 cup soy sauce
¼ cup sugar
2 tablespoons lime juice
½ cup mirin
¼ teaspoon red pepper flakes, crushed
¼ cup orange juice
¼ teaspoon ginger, grated
1 garlic clove, minced

DIRECTIONS:

1.Put soy sauce in a pan, heat up over medium heat, add mirin, sugar, lime and orange juice, pepper flakes, ginger and garlic, stir well, bring to a boil and take off heat.

2.Transfer half of the marinade to a bowl, add halibut, toss to coat and leave aside in the fridge for 30 minutes.

3.Transfer halibut to your air fryer and cook at 390 0 F for 10 minutes, flipping once.

4.Divide halibut steaks on plates, drizzle the rest of the marinade all over and serve hot.

Enjoy!

Nutrition: calories 286, fat 5, fiber 12, carbs 14, protein 23

SECTION SIX

Vegetable Recipes

Thyme and Parsley Salmon

SERVING	PREP TIME	COOK TIME
4	10 MINS	15 MINS

INGREDIENTS:

4 salmon fillets, boneless
Juice from 1 lemon
1 yellow onion, chopped
3 tomatoes, sliced
4 thyme springs
4 parsley springs
3 tablespoons extra virgin olive oil
Salt and black pepper to the taste

DIRECTIONS:

1.Drizzle 1 tablespoon oil in a pan that fits your air fryer,, add a layer of tomatoes, salt and pepper, drizzle 1 more tablespoon oil, add fish, season them with salt and pepper, drizzle the rest of the oil, add thyme and parsley springs, onions, lemon juice, salt and pepper, place in your air fryer's basket and cook at 360 0 F for 12 minutes shaking once.

2.Divide everything on plates and serve right away.

Enjoy!

Nutrition: calories 242, fat 9, fiber 12, carbs 20, protein 31

Trout and Butter Sauce

SERVING	PREP TIME	COOK TIME
4	10 MINS	10 MINS

INGREDIENTS:

4 trout fillets, boneless
Salt and black pepper to the taste
3 teaspoons lemon zest, grated
3 tablespoons chives, chopped
6 tablespoons butter
2 tablespoons olive oil
2 teaspoons lemon juice

DIRECTIONS:

1.Season trout with salt and pepper, drizzle the olive oil, rub, transfer to your air fryer and cook at 360 0 F for 10 minutes, flipping once.

2.Meanwhile, heat up a pan with the butter over medium heat, add salt, pepper, chives, lemon juice and zest, whisk well, cook for 1-2 minutes and take off heat

3.Divide fish fillets on plates, drizzle butter sauce all over and serve.

Enjoy!

Nutrition: calories 300, fat 12, fiber 9, carbs 27, protein 24

Salmon and Avocado Salsa

SERVING	PREP TIME	COOK TIME
4	30 MINS	10 MINS

INGREDIENTS:

4 salmon fillets
1 tablespoon olive oil
Salt and black pepper to the taste
1 teaspoon cumin, ground
1 teaspoon sweet paprika
½ teaspoon chili powder
1 teaspoon garlic powder
For the salsa:
1 small red onion, chopped
1 avocado, pitted, peeled and chopped
2 tablespoons cilantro, chopped
Juice from 2 limes
Salt and black pepper to the taste

DIRECTIONS:

1.In a bowl, mix salt, pepper, chili powder, onion powder, paprika and cumin, stir, rub salmon with this mix, drizzle the oil, rub again, transfer to your air fryer and cook at 350 0 F for 5 minutes on each side.

2.Meanwhile, in a bowl, mix avocado with red onion, salt, pepper, cilantro and lime juice and stir.

3.Divide fillets on plates, top with avocado salsa and serve.

Enjoy!

Nutrition: calories 300, fat 14, fiber 4, carbs 18, protein 16

Italian Barramundi Fillets and Tomato Salsa

SERVING	PREP TIME	COOK TIME
4	10 MINS	8 MINS

INGREDIENTS:

2 barramundi fillets, boneless
1 tablespoon olive oil+ 2 teaspoons
2 teaspoons Italian seasoning
¼ cup green olives, pitted and chopped
¼ cup cherry tomatoes, chopped
¼ cup black olives, chopped
1 tablespoon lemon zest
2 tablespoons lemon zest
Salt and black pepper to the taste
2 tablespoons parsley, chopped

DIRECTIONS:

1.Rub fish with salt, pepper, Italian seasoning and 2 teaspoons olive oil, transfer to your air fryer and cook at 360 0 F for 8 minutes, flipping them halfway.

2.In a bowl, mix tomatoes with black olives, green olives, salt, pepper, lemon zest and lemon juice, parsley and 1 tablespoon olive oil and toss well

3.Divide fish on plates, add tomato salsa on top and serve.

Enjoy!

Nutrition: calories 270, fat 4, fiber 2, carbs 18, protein 2

Tuna and Chimichuri Sauce

SERVING	PREP TIME	COOK TIME
4	10 MINS	8 MINS

INGREDIENTS:

½ cup cilantro, chopped
1/3 cup olive oil+ 2 tablespoons
1 small red onion, chopped
3 tablespoon balsamic vinegar
2 tablespoons parsley, chopped
2 tablespoons basil, chopped
1 jalapeno pepper, chopped
1 pound sushi tuna steak
Salt and black pepper to the taste
1 teaspoon red pepper flakes
1 teaspoon thyme, chopped
3 garlic cloves, minced
2 avocados, pitted, peeled and sliced
6 ounces baby arugula

DIRECTIONS:

1.In a bowl, mix 1/3 cup oil with jalapeno, vinegar, onion, cilantro, basil, garlic, parsley, pepper flakes, thyme, salt and pepper, whisk well and leave aside for now.

2.Season tuna with salt and pepper, rub with the rest of the oil, place in your air fryer and cook at 360 0 F for 3 minutes on each side.

3.Mix arugula with half of the chimichuri mix you've made and toss to coat.

4.Divide arugula on plates, slice tuna and also divide among plates, top with the rest of the chimichuri and serve.

Enjoy!

Nutrition: calories 276, fat 3, fiber 1, carbs 14, protein 20

Squid and Guacamole

SERVING	PREP TIME	COOK TIME
2	10 MINS	6 MINS

INGREDIENTS:

2 medium squids, tentacles separated and tubes scored lengthwise
1 tablespoon olive oil
Juice from 1 lime
Salt and black pepper to the taste
For the guacamole:
2 avocados, pitted, peeled and chopped
1 tablespoon coriander, chopped
2 red chilies, chopped
1 tomato, chopped
1 red onion, chopped
Juice from 2 limes

DIRECTIONS:

1.Season squid and squid tentacles with salt, pepper, drizzle the olive oil all over, put in the air fryer's basket and then cook at 360 0 F for 3 minutes on each side.

2.Transfer squid to a bowl, drizzle lime juice all over and toss.

3.Meanwhile, put avocado in a bowl, mash with a fork, add coriander, chilies, tomato, onion and juice from 2 limes and toss.

4.Divide squid on plates, top with guacamole and serve.

Enjoy!

Nutrition: calories 500, fat 43, fiber 6, carbs 7, protein 20

Shrimp and Cauliflower

SERVING	PREP TIME	COOK TIME
2	10 MINS	12 MINS

INGREDIENTS:

1 tablespoon butter
Cooking spray
1 cauliflower head, riced
1 pound shrimp, peeled and deveined
¼ cup heavy cream
8 ounces mushrooms, roughly chopped
A pinch of red pepper flakes
Salt and black pepper to the taste
2 garlic cloves, minced
4 bacon slices, cooked and crumbled
½ cup beef stock
1 tablespoon parsley, finely chopped
1 tablespoon chives, chopped

DIRECTIONS:

1.Season shrimp with salt and pepper, spray with cooking oil, place in your air fryer and cook at 360 0 F for 7 minutes.

2.mushrooms, stir and cook for 3-4 minutes.

3.Add garlic, cauliflower rice, pepper flakes, stock, cream, chives, parsley, salt and pepper, stir, cook for a few minutes and take off heat.

4.Divide shrimp on plates, add cauliflower mix on the side, sprinkle bacon on top and serve.

Enjoy!

Nutrition: calories 245, fat 7, fiber 4, carbs 6, protein 20

Stuffed Salmon

SERVING	PREP TIME	COOK TIME
2	10 MINS	20 MINS

INGREDIENTS:

2 salmon fillets, skinless and boneless
1 tablespoon olive oil
5 ounces tiger shrimp, peeled, deveined and chopped
6 mushrooms, chopped
3 green onions, chopped
2 cups spinach, torn
¼ cup macadamia nuts, toasted and chopped
Blackpepper and salt

DIRECTIONS:

1.Heat up the oil in a pan over medium high heat, add mushrooms, onions, salt and pepper, stir and cook for 4 minutes.

2.Add macadamia nuts, spinach and shrimp, stir, cook for 3 minutes and take off heat.

3.Make an incision lengthwise in each salmon fillet, season with salt and pepper, divide spinach and shrimp mix into incisions and rub with the rest of the olive oil.

4.Place in your air fryer's basket and cook at 360 0 F and cook for 10 minutes, flipping halfway.

5.Divide stuffed salmon on plates and serve.

Enjoy!

Nutrition: calories 290, fat 15, fiber 3, carbs 12, protein 31

Flavored Jamaican Salmon

SERVING	PREP TIME	COOK TIME
4	10 MINS	10 MINS

INGREDIENTS:

2 teaspoons sriracha sauce
4 teaspoons sugar
3 scallions, chopped
Salt and black pepper to the taste
2 teaspoons olive oil
4 teaspoons apple cider vinegar
3 teaspoons avocado oil
4 medium salmon fillets, boneless
4 cups baby arugula
2 cups cabbage, shredded
1 and ½ teaspoon Jamaican jerk seasoning ¼ cup pepitas, toasted
2 cups radish, julienned

DIRECTIONS:

1.In a bowl, mix sriracha with sugar, whisk and transfer 2 teaspoons to another bowl.

2.Combine 2 teaspoons sriracha mix with the avocado oil, olive oil, vinegar, salt and pepper and whisk well.

3.Sprinkle jerk seasoning over salmon, rub with sriracha and sugar mix and season with salt and pepper.

4.Transfer to your air fryer and cook at 360 0 F for 10 minutes, flipping once.

5.In a bowl, mix radishes with cabbage, arugula, salt, pepper, sriracha and vinegar mix and toss well.

6.Divide salmon and radish mix on plates, sprinkle pepitas and scallions on top and serve.

Enjoy!

Nutrition: calories 290, fat 6, fiber 12, carbs 17, protein 10

Salmon and Orange Marmalade

SERVING	PREP TIME	COOK TIME
4	10 MINS	15 MINS

INGREDIENTS:

1 pound wild salmon, skinless, boneless and cubed
2 lemons, sliced
¼ cup balsamic vinegar
¼ cup orange juice
1/3 cup orange marmalade
A pinch of salt and black pepper

DIRECTIONS:

1.Heat up a pot with the vinegar over medium heat, add marmalade and orange juice, stir, bring to a simmer, cook for 1 minute and take off heat.

2.Thread salmon cubes and lemon slices on skewers, season with salt and black pepper, brush them with half of the orange marmalade mix, arrange in your air fryer's basket and cook at 360 0 F for 3 minutes on each side.

3.Brush skewers with the rest of the vinegar mix, divide among plates and serve right away with a side salad.

Enjoy!

Nutrition: calories 240, fat 9, fiber 12, carbs 14, protein 10

Chili Salmon

SERVING	PREP TIME	COOK TIME
12	10 MINS	15 MINS

INGREDIENTS:

1 and ¼ cups coconut, shredded
1 pound salmon, cubed
1/3 cup flour
A pinch of salt and black pepper
1 egg
2 tablespoons olive oil
¼ cup water
4 red chilies, chopped
3 garlic cloves, minced
¼ cup balsamic vinegar
½ cup honey

DIRECTIONS:

1.In a bowl, mix flour with a pinch of salt and stir.

2.In another bowl, mix egg with black pepper and whisk.

3.Put coconut in a third bowl.

4.Dip salmon cubes in flour, egg and coconut, put them in your air fryer's basket, cook at 370 0 F for 8 minutes, shaking halfway and divide among plates.

5.Heat up the water inside a pan over medium high heat, add chilies, cloves, vinegar and honey, stir very well, bring to a boil, simmer for a couple of minutes, drizzle over salmon and serve.

Enjoy!

Nutrition: calories 220, fat 12, fiber 2, carbs 14, protein 13

Salmon and Avocado Sauce

SERVING	PREP TIME	COOK TIME
4	10 MINS	10 MINS

INGREDIENTS:

1 avocado, pitted, peeled and chopped
4 salmon fillets, boneless
¼ cup cilantro, chopped
1/3 cup coconut milk
1 tablespoon lime juice
1 tablespoon lime zest, grated
1 teaspoon onion powder
1 teaspoon garlic powder
Salt and black pepper to the taste

DIRECTIONS:

1.Season salmon fillets with salt, black pepper and lime zest, rub well, put in your air fryer, cook at 350 0 F for 9 minutes, flipping once and divide among plates.

2.In your food processor, mix avocado with cilantro, garlic powder, onion powder, lime juice, salt, pepper and coconut milk, blend well, drizzle over salmon and serve right away.

Enjoy!

Nutrition: calories 260, fat 7, fiber 20, carbs 28, protein 18

Salmon and Chives Vinaigrette

SERVING	PREP TIME	COOK TIME
4	10 MINS	12 MINS

INGREDIENTS:

2 tablespoons dill, chopped
4 salmon fillets, boneless
2 tablespoons chives, chopped
1/3 cup maple syrup
1 tablespoon olive oil
3 tablespoons balsamic vinegar
Salt and black pepper to the taste

DIRECTIONS:

1.Season the fish with pepper, salt and rub with the oil, place in your air fryer and cook at 350 0 F for 8 minutes, flipping once.

2.Heat up a small pot with the vinegar over medium heat, add maple syrup, chives and dill, stir and cook for 3 minutes.

3.Divide fish on plates and serve with chives vinaigrette on top.⌧

Enjoy!

Nutrition: calories 270, fat 3, fiber 13, carbs 25, protein 10

SECTION SEVEN

Herbed Chicken

SERVING	PREP TIME	COOK TIME
4	30 MINS	40 MINS

INGREDIENTS:

1 whole chicken
Salt and black pepper to the taste
1 teaspoon garlic powder
1 teaspoon onion powder
½ teaspoon thyme, dried
1 teaspoon rosemary, dried
1 tablespoon lemon juice
2 tablespoons olive oil

DIRECTIONS:

1.Season the chicken with pepper and salt, rub with thyme, rosemary, garlic powder and onion powder, rub with lemon juice and olive oil and leave aside for 30 minutes.

2.Put chicken in your air fryer and cook at 360 0 F for 20 minutes on each side.

3.Leave chicken aside to cool down, carve and serve.

Enjoy!

Nutrition: calories 390, fat 10, fiber 5, carbs 22, protein 20

Chicken Parmesan

SERVING	PREP TIME	COOK TIME
4	10 MINS	15 MINS

INGREDIENTS:

2 cups panko bread crumbs
¼ cup parmesan, grated
½ teaspoon garlic powder
2 cups white flour
1 egg, whisked
1 and ½ pounds chicken cutlets, skinless and boneless Salt and black pepper to the taste
1 cup mozzarella, grated
2 cups tomato sauce
3 tablespoons basil, chopped

DIRECTIONS:

1.In a bowl, mix panko with parmesan and garlic powder and stir.

2.Put flour in a second bowl and the egg in a third.

3.Season chicken with salt and pepper, dip in flour, then in egg mix and in panko.

4.Put chicken pieces in your air fryer and cook them at 360 0 F for 3 minutes on each side.

5.Transfer chicken to a baking dish that fits your air fryer, add tomato sauce and top with mozzarella, introduce in your air fryer and cook at 375 0 F for 7 minutes.

6.Divide among plates, sprinkle basil on top and serve.

Enjoy!

Nutrition: calories 304, fat 12, fiber 11, carbs 22, protein 15

Chinese Duck Legs

SERVING	PREP TIME	COOK TIME
2	10 MINS	36 MINS

INGREDIENTS:

2 duck legs
2 dried chilies, chopped
1 tablespoon olive oil
2 star anise
1 bunch spring onions, chopped
4 ginger slices
1 tablespoon oyster sauce
1 tablespoon soy sauce
1 teaspoon sesame oil
14 ounces water
1 tablespoon rice wine

DIRECTIONS:

1.Heat up the oil ina pan over medium high heat, add chili, star anise, sesame oil, rice wine, ginger, oyster sauce, soy sauce and water, stir and cook for 6 minutes.

2.Add spring onions and duck legs, toss to coat, transfer to a pan that fits your air fryer, put in your air fryer and cook at 370 0 F for 30 minutes.

3.Divide among plates and serve.

Enjoy!

Nutrition: calories 300, fat 12, fiber 12, carbs 26, protein 18

Chinese Stuffed Chicken

SERVING	PREP TIME	COOK TIME
8	10 MINS	35 MINS

INGREDIENTS:

1 whole chicken
10 wolfberries
2 red chilies, chopped
4 ginger slices
1 yam, cubed
1 teaspoon soy sauce
Salt and white pepper to the taste
3 teaspoons sesame oil

DIRECTIONS:

1.Season chicken with salt, pepper, rub with soy sauce and sesame oil and stuff with wolfberries, yam cubes, chilies and ginger.

2.Place in your air fryer, cook at 400 0 F for 20 minutes and then at 360 0 F for 15 minutes.

3.Carve chicken, divide among plates and serve.

Enjoy!

Nutrition: calories 320, fat 12, fiber 17, carbs 22, protein 12

Chicken and Capers

SERVING	PREP TIME	COOK TIME
2	10 MINS	20 MINS

INGREDIENTS:

4 chicken thighs
3 tablespoons capers
4 garlic cloves, minced
3 tablespoons butter, melted
Salt and black pepper to the taste
½ cup chicken stock
1 lemon, sliced
4 green onions, chopped

DIRECTIONS:

1.Brush chicken with butter, sprinkle salt and pepper to the taste, place them in a baking dish that fits your air fryer.

2.Also add capers, garlic, chicken stock and lemon slices, toss to coat, introduce in your air fryer and cook at 370 0 F for 20 minutes, shaking halfway.

3.Sprinkle green onions, divide among plates and serve.

Enjoy!

Nutrition: calories 200, fat 9, fiber 10, carbs 17, protein 7

Chicken and Black Olives Sauce

SERVING	PREP TIME	COOK TIME
2	10 MINS	8 MINS

INGREDIENTS:

1 chicken breast cut into 4 pieces
2 tablespoons olive oil
3 garlic cloves, minced
For the sauce:
1 cup black olives, pitted
Salt and black pepper to the taste
2 tablespoons olive oil
¼ cup parsley, chopped
1 tablespoons lemon juice

DIRECTIONS:

1.In your food processor, mix olives with salt, pepper, 2 tablespoons olive oil, lemon juice and parsley, blend very well and transfer to a bowl.

2.Season the chicken with pepper and salt, rub with the oil and garlic, place in your preheated air fryer and cook at 3700F for 8 minutes.

3.Divide chicken on plates, top with olives sauce and serve.

Enjoy!

Nutrition: calories 270, fat 12, fiber 12, carbs 23, protein 22

Pepperoni Chicken

SERVING	PREP TIME	COOK TIME
6	10 MINS	22 MINS

INGREDIENTS:

1 tablespoon olive oil
14 ouces tomato paste
4 medium chicken breasts, skinless
Black pepper and Salt
1 teaspoon oregano, dried
6 ounces mozzarella, sliced
2 ounces sliced pepperoni
1 teaspoon garli powder

DIRECTIONS:

1.Mix the chicken with salt, pepper, garlic powder and oregano and toss in a bowl.

2.Put chicken in the air fryer and cook at 3500F for six minutes and put to a pan that sizes your air fryer.

3.Add the mozzarella slices on top, spread tomato paste, top with pepperoni slices, introduce in your air fryer and cook at 3500 F for fifteen minutes more.

4.Share among plates and serve.

Enjoy!

Nutrition: calories 320, fat 10, fiber 16, carbs 23, protein 27

Turkey Quarters and Veggies

SERVING	PREP TIME	COOK TIME
4	10 MINS	34 MINS

INGREDIENTS:

1 yellow onion, chopped
1 carrot, chopped
3 garlic cloves, minced
2 pounds turkey quarters
1 celery stalk, chopped
1 cup chicken stock
2 tablespoons olive oil
2 bay leaves
½ teaspoon rosemary, dried
½ teaspoon sage, dried
½ teaspoon thyme, dried
Salt and black pepper to the taste

DIRECTIONS:

1.Rub turkey quarters with salt, pepper, half of the oil, thyme, sage, rosemary and thyme, put inside the air fryer and cook at 360 0 F for 20 minutes.

2.In a pan that sizes your air fryer, mix onion with carrot, garlic, celery, the rest of the oil, stock, bay leaves, salt and pepper and toss.

3.Add turkey, introduce everything in your air fryer and cook at 360 0 F for 14 minutes more.

4.Divide everything on plates and serve.

Enjoy!

Nutrition: calories 362, fat 12, fiber 16, carbs 22, protein 17

Chicken and Garlic Sauce

SERVING	PREP TIME	COOK TIME
4	10 MINS	20 MINS

INGREDIENTS:

1 tablespoon butter, melted
4 chicken breasts, skin on and bone-in
1 tablespoon olive oil
Salt and black pepper to the taste
40 garlic cloves, peeled and chopped
2 thyme springs
¼ cup chicken stock
2 tablespoons parsley, chopped
¼ cup dry white wine

DIRECTIONS:

1.Season the chicken breasts using pepper and salt, rub with the oil, place in your air fryer, cook at 360 0 F for 4 minutes on each side and transfer to a heat proof dish that fits your air fryer.

2.Add melted butter, garlic, thyme, stock, wine and parsley, toss, introduce in your air fryer and cook at 350 0 F for 15 minutes more.

3.Divide everything on plates and serve.

Enjoy!

Nutrition: calories 227, fat 9, fiber 13, carbs 22, protein 12

Turkey, Peas and Mushrooms Casserole

SERVING	PREP TIME	COOK TIME
4	10 MINS	20 MINS

INGREDIENTS:

2 pounds turkey breasts, skinless, boneless Salt and black pepper to the taste
1 yellow onion, chopped
1 celery stalk, chopped
½ cup peas
1 cup chicken stock
1 cup cream of mushrooms soup
1 cup bread cubes

DIRECTIONS:

1.In a pan that sizes your air fryer, mix turkey with salt, pepper, onion, celery, peas and stock, introduce in your air fryer and cook at 360 0 F for 15 minutes.

2.Add bread cubes and cream of mushroom soup, stir toss and cook at 360 0 F for 5 minutes more.

3.Divide among plates and serve hot.

Enjoy!

Nutrition: calories 271, fat 9, fiber 9, carbs 16, protein 7

Chicken and Apricot Sauce

SERVING	PREP TIME	COOK TIME
4	10 MINS	20 MINS

INGREDIENTS:

1 whole chicken, sliced
Salt and black pepper
1 tablespoon olive oil
½ teaspoon smoked paprika
¼ cup white wine
½ teaspoon marjoram, dried
¼ cup chicken stock
2 tablespoons white vinegar
¼ cup apricot preserves
1 and ½ teaspoon ginger, grated
2 tablespoons honey

DIRECTIONS:

1.Season chicken with salt, pepper, marjoram and paprika, toss to coat, add oil, rub well, place in the air fryer and cook at 360 0 F for 10 minutes.

2.Transfer chicken to a pan that fits your air fryer, add stock, wine, vinegar, ginger, apricot preserves and honey, toss, put in your air fryer and cook at 360 0 F for 10 minutes more.

3.Divide chicken and apricot sauce on plates and serve.

Enjoy!

Nutrition: calories 200, fat 7, fiber 19, carbs 20, protein 14

SECTION EIGHT

Appetizers

Beets and Arugula Salad

SERVING	PREP TIME	COOK TIME
4	20 MINS	10 MINS

INGREDIENTS:

1 and ½ pounds beets, peeled and quartered A drizzle of olive oil
2 teaspoons orange zest, grated
2 tablespoons cider vinegar
½ cup orange juice
2 tablespoons brown sugar
2 scallions, chopped
2 teaspoons mustard
2 cups arugula

DIRECTIONS:

1.Rub beets with the oil and orange juice, place them in your air fryer and cook at 350 0 F for 10 minutes.

2.Transfer beet quarters to a bowl, add scallions, arugula and orange zest and toss.

3.In a separate bowl, mix sugar with mustard and vinegar, whisk well, add to salad, toss and serve.

Enjoy it!

Nutrition: calories 121, fat 2, fiber 3, carbs 11, protein 4

Sweet Baby Carrots Dish

SERVING	PREP TIME	COOK TIME
4	10 MINS	10 MINS

INGREDIENTS:

2 cups baby carrots
A pinch of salt and black pepper
1 tablespoon brown sugar
½ tablespoon butter, melted

DIRECTIONS:

1.In the dish that fits your air fryer, mix baby carrots with butter, salt, pepper and sugar, toss, introduce in your air fryer and cook at 350 0 F for 10 minutes.

2.Divide among plates and serve.

Enjoy it!

Nutrition: calories 100, fat 2, fiber 3, carbs 7, protein 4

Collard Greens Mix

SERVING	PREP TIME	COOK TIME
4	10 MINS	10 MINS

INGREDIENTS:

1 bunch collard greens, trimmed
2 tablespoons olive oil
2 tablespoons tomato puree
1 yellow onion, chopped
3 garlic cloves, minced
Salt and black pepper to the taste
1 tablespoon balsamic vinegar
1 teaspoon sugar

DIRECTIONS:

1.In the dish that fits your air fryer, mix oil, garlic, vinegar, onion and tomato puree and whisk.

2.Add collard greens, salt, pepper and sugar, toss, introduce in your air fryer and cook at 320 0 F for 10 minutes.

3.Divide collard greens mix on plates and serve.

Enjoy!

Nutrition: calories 121, fat 3, fiber 3, carbs 7, protein 3

Collard Greens and Turkey Wings

SERVING	PREP TIME	COOK TIME
6	10 MINS	20 MINS

INGREDIENTS:

1 sweet onion, chopped
2 smoked turkey wings
2 tablespoons olive oil
3 garlic cloves, minced
2 and ½ pounds collard greens, chopped
Salt and black pepper to the taste
2 tablespoons apple cider vinegar
1 tablespoon brown sugar
½ teaspoon crushed red pepper

DIRECTIONS:

1.Heating up a pan that fits your air fryer with the oil over medium high heat, add onions, stir and cook for 2 minutes.

2.Add garlic, greens, vinegar, salt, pepper, crushed red pepper, sugar and smoked turkey, introduce in preheated air fryer and cook at 350 0 F for 15 minutes.

3.Divide greens and turkey on plates and serve.

Enjoy!

Nutrition: calories 262, fat 4, fiber 8, carbs 12, protein 4

Herbed
Eggplant and Zucchini Mix

SERVING	PREP TIME	COOK TIME
4	10 MINS	8 MINS

INGREDIENTS:

1 eggplant, roughly cubed
3 zucchinis, roughly cubed
2 tablespoons lemon juice
Salt and black pepper to the taste
1 teaspoon thyme, dried
1 teaspoon oregano, dried
3 tablespoons olive oil

DIRECTIONS:

1.Put eggplant in a dish that fits your air fryer, add zucchinis, lemon juice, salt, pepper, thyme, oregano and olive oil, toss, introduce in your air fryer and cook at 360 0 F for 8 minutes.

2.Divide among plates and serve right away.

Enjoy!

Nutrition: calories 152, fat 5, fiber 7, carbs 19, protein 5

Crispy Potatoes and Parsley

SERVING	PREP TIME	COOK TIME
4	10 MINS	10 MINS

INGREDIENTS:

1 pound gold potatoes, cut into wedges
Salt and black pepper to the taste
2 tablespoons olive
Juice from ½ lemon
¼ cup parsley leaves, chopped

DIRECTIONS:

1.Rub potatoes with salt, pepper, lemon juice and olive oil, put them in your air fryer and cook at 350 0 F for 10 minutes.

2.Divide among plates, sprinkle parsley on top and serve.

Enjoy!

Nutrition: calories 152, fat 3, fiber 7, carbs 17, protein 4

Swiss Chard and Sausage

SERVING	PREP TIME	COOK TIME
8	10 MINS	20 MINS

INGREDIENTS:

8 cups Swiss chard, chopped
½ cup onion, chopped
1 tablespoon olive oil
1 garlic clove, minced
Salt and black pepper to the taste
3 eggs
2 cups ricotta cheese
1 cup mozzarella, shredded
A pinch of nutmeg
¼ cup parmesan, grated
1 pound sausage, chopped

DIRECTIONS:

1.Heating a pan that fits your air fryer with the oil over medium heat, add onions, garlic, Swiss chard, salt, pepper and nutmeg, stir, cook for 2 minutes and take off heat.

2.In a bowl, whisk eggs with mozzarella, parmesan and ricotta, stir, pour over Swiss chard mix, toss, introduce in your air fryer and cook at 320 0 F for 17 minutes.

3.Divide among plates and serve.

Enjoy!

Nutrition: calories 332, fat 13, fiber 3, carbs 14, protein 23

Flavored Air Fried Tomatoes

SERVING	PREP TIME	COOK TIME
8	10 MINS	15 MINS

INGREDIENTS:

1 jalapeno pepper, chopped
4 garlic cloves, minced
2 pounds cherry tomatoes, halved
Salt and black pepper to the taste
¼ cup olive oil
½ teaspoon oregano, dried
¼ cup basil, chopped
½ cup parmesan, grated

DIRECTIONS:

1.In a bowl, mix tomatoes with garlic, jalapeno, season with salt, pepper and oregano and drizzle the oil, toss to coat, introduce in your air fryer and cook at 380 0 F for 15 minutes.

2.Transfer tomatoes to a bowl, add basil and parmesan, toss and serve.

Enjoy it!

Nutrition: calories 140, fat 2, fiber 2, carbs 6, protein 8

Italian Eggplant Stew

SERVING	PREP TIME	COOK TIME
4	10 MINS	15 MINS

INGREDIENTS:

1 red onion, chopped
2 garlic cloves, chopped
1 bunch parsley, chopped
Salt and black pepper to the taste
1 teaspoon oregano, dried
2 eggplants, cut into medium chunks
2 tablespoons olive oil
2 tablespoons capers, chopped
1 handful green olives, pitted and sliced
5 tomatoes, chopped
3 tablespoons herb vinegar

DIRECTIONS:

1.Heat up a pan that fits your air fryer with the oil over medium heat, add eggplant, oregano, salt and pepper, stir and cook for 5 minutes.

2.Add garlic, onion, parsley, capers, olives, vinegar and tomatoes, stir, introduce in your air fryer and cook at 360 0 F for 15 minutes.

3.Divide into bowls and serve.

Enjoy!

Nutrition: calories 170, fat 13, fiber 3, carbs 5, protein 7

Tomato and Basil Tart

SERVING	PREP TIME	COOK TIME
2	10 MINS	14 MINS

INGREDIENTS:

1 bunch basil, chopped
4 eggs
1 garlic clove, minced
Salt and black pepper to the taste
½ cup cherry tomatoes, halved
¼ cup cheddar cheese, grated

DIRECTIONS:

1.In a bowl, mix eggs with salt, black pepper, cheese and basil and whisk well.

2.Pour this into a baking dish that fits your air fryer, arrange tomatoes on top, introduce in the fryer and cook at 320 0 F for 14 minutes.

3.Slice and serve right away.

Enjoy it!

Nutrition: calories 140, fat 1, fiber 1, carbs 2, protein 10

Eggplant and Garlic Sauce

SERVING	PREP TIME	COOK TIME
4	10 MINS	10 MINS

INGREDIENTS:

2 tablespoons olive oil
2 garlic cloves, minced
3 eggplants, halved and sliced
1 red chili pepper, chopped
1 green onion stalk, chopped
1 tablespoon ginger, grated
1 tablespoon soy sauce
1 tablespoon balsamic vinegar

DIRECTIONS:

1.Heating a pan that fits your air fryer with the oil over medium high heat, add eggplant slices and cook for 2 minutes.

2.Add chili pepper, garlic, green onions, ginger, soy sauce and vinegar, introduce in your air fryer and cook at 320 0 F for 7 minutes.

3.Divide among plates and serve.

Enjoy!

Nutrition: calories 130, fat 2, fiber 4, carbs 7, protein 9

Delicious Creamy Green Beans

SERVING	PREP TIME	COOK TIME
4	10 MINS	15 MINS

INGREDIENTS:

½ cup heavy cream
1 cup mozzarella, shredded
2/3 cup parmesan, grated
Salt and black pepper to the taste
2 pounds green beans
2 teaspoons lemon zest, grated
A pinch of red pepper flakes

DIRECTIONS:

1.Put the beans in a dish that fits your air fryer, add heavy cream, salt, pepper, lemon zest, pepper flakes, mozzarella and parmesan, toss, introduce in your air fryer and cook at 350 0 F for 15 minutes.

2.Divide among plates and serve right away.

Enjoy!

Nutrition: calories 231, fat 6, fiber 7, carbs 8, protein 5

Green Beans and Tomatoes

SERVING	PREP TIME	COOK TIME
4	10 MINS	15 MINS

INGREDIENTS:

1 pint cherry tomatoes
1 pound green beans
2 tablespoons olive oil
Salt and black pepper to the taste

DIRECTIONS:

1.In a bowl, mix cherry tomatoes with green beans, olive oil, salt and pepper, toss, transfer to your air fryer and cook at 400 0 F for 15 minutes.

2.Divide among plates and serve right away.

Enjoy it!

Nutrition: calories 162, fat 6, fiber 5, carbs 8, protein 9

Easy Green Beans and Potatoes

SERVING	PREP TIME	COOK TIME
5	10 MINS	15 MINS

INGREDIENTS:

2 pounds green beans
6 new potatoes, halved
Salt and black pepper to the taste
A drizzle of olive oil
6 bacon slices, cooked and chopped

DIRECTIONS:

1.In a bowl, mix green beans with potatoes, salt, pepper and oil, toss, transfer to your air fryer and cook at 390 0 F for 15 minutes.

2.Divide among plates and serve with bacon sprinkled on top.

Enjoy!

Nutrition: calories 374, fat 15, fiber 12, carbs 28, protein 12

Flavored Green Beans

SERVING	PREP TIME	COOK TIME
4	10 MINS	15 MINS

INGREDIENTS:

1 pound red potatoes, cut into wedges
1 pound green beans
2 garlic cloves, minced
2 tablespoons olive oil
Salt and black pepper to the taste
½ teaspoon oregano, dried

DIRECTIONS:

1.In a pan that sizes your air fryer, combine potatoes with green beans, garlic, oil, salt, pepper and oregano, toss, introduce in your air fryer and cook at 380 0 F for 15 minutes.

2.Divide among plates and serve.

Enjoy!

Nutrition: calories 211, fat 6, fiber 7, carbs 8, protein 5

Bread Pudding

SERVING	PREP TIME	COOK TIME
4	10 MINS	1 HOUR

INGREDIENTS:

6 glazed doughnuts, crumbled
1 cup cherries
4 egg yolks
1 and ½ cups whipping cream
½ cup raisins
¼ cup sugar
½ cup chocolate chips.

DIRECTIONS:

1.In a bowl, mix cherries with egg yolks and whipping cream and stir well.

2.In another bowl, mix raisins with sugar, chocolate chips and doughnuts and stir.

3.Combine the 2 mixtures, transfer everything to a greased pan that fits your air fryer and cook at 310 0 F for 1 hour.

4.Chill pudding before cutting and serving it.

Enjoy!

Nutrition: calories 302, fat 8, fiber 2, carbs 23, protein 10

SECTION NINE

Deserts

Apple Bread

SERVING	PREP TIME	COOK TIME
6	10 MINS	40 MINS

INGREDIENTS:

3 cups apples, cored and cubed
1 cup sugar
1 tablespoon vanilla
2 eggs
1 tablespoon apple pie spice
2 cups white flour
1 tablespoon baking powder
1 stick butter
1 cup water

DIRECTIONS:

1.In a bowl mix egg with 1 butter stick, apple pie spice and sugar and stir using your mixer.

2.Add apples and stir again well.

3.In another bowl, mix baking powder with flour and stir.

4.Combine the 2 mixtures, stir and pour into a spring form pan.

5.Put spring form pan in your air fryer and cook at 320 0 F for 40 minutes

6.Slice and serve.

Enjoy!

Nutrition: calories 192, fat 6, fiber 7, carbs 14, protein 7

Banana Bread

SERVING	PREP TIME	COOK TIME
6	10 MINS	40 MINS

INGREDIENTS:

¾ cup sugar
1/3 cup butter
1 teaspoon vanilla extract
1 egg
2 bananas, mashed
1 teaspoon baking powder
1 and ½ cups flour
½ teaspoons baking soda
1/3 cup milk
1 and ½ teaspoons cream of tartar
Cooking spray

DIRECTIONS:

1.In a bowl, mix milk with cream of tartar, sugar, butter, egg, vanilla and bananas and stir everything.

2.In a different bowl, mix the flour together with baking soda and baking powder.

3.Combine the 2 mixtures, stir well, pour this into a cake pan greased with some cooking spray, introduce in your air fryer and cook at 3200F for 40 minutes.

4.Take bread out, leave aside to cool down, slice and serve it.

Enjoy!

Nutrition: calories 292, fat 7, fiber 8, carbs 28, protein 4

Lime Cheesecake

SERVING	PREP TIME	COOK TIME
10	4 HOURS + 10 MINS	4 MINS

INGREDIENTS:

2 tablespoons butter, melted
2 teaspoons sugar
4 ounces flour
¼ cup coconut, shredded
For the filling:
1 pound cream cheese
Zest from 1 lime, grated
Juice form 1 lime
2 cups hot water
2 sachets lime jelly

DIRECTIONS:

1.In a bowl, mix coconut with flour, butter and sugar, stir well and press this on the bottom of a pan that fits your air fryer.

2.Meanwhile, put the hot water in a bowl, add jelly sachets and stir until it dissolves.

3.Put cream cheese in a bowl, add jelly, lime juice and zest and whisk really well.

4.Add this over the crust, spread, introduce in the air fryer and cook at 300 0 F for 4 minutes.

5.Keep in the fridge for 4 hours before serving.

Enjoy!

Nutrition: calories 260, fat 23, fiber 2, carbs 5, protein 7

Easy Granola

SERVING	PREP TIME	COOK TIME
4	10 MINS	35 MINS

INGREDIENTS:

1 cup coconut, shredded
½ cup almonds
½ cup pecans, chopped
2 tablespoons sugar
½ cup pumpkin seeds
½ cup sunflower seeds
2 tablespoons sunflower oil
1 teaspoon nutmeg, ground
1 teaspoon apple pie spice mix

DIRECTIONS:

1.In a bowl, mix almonds and pecans with pumpkin seeds, sunflower seeds, coconut, nutmeg and apple pie spice mix and stir well.

2.Heating a pan with the oil over medium heat, add sugar and stir well.

3.Pour this over nuts and coconut mix and stir well.

4.Spread this on a lined baking sheet that fits your air fryer, introduce in your air fryer and cook at 300 0 F and bake for 25 minutes.

5.Leave your granola to cool down, cut and serve.

Enjoy!

Nutrition: calories 322, fat 7, fiber 8, carbs 12, protein 7

Strawberry Cobbler

SERVING	PREP TIME	COOK TIME
6	10 MINS	25 MINS

INGREDIENTS:

¾ cup sugar
6 cups strawberries, halved
1/8 teaspoon baking powder
1 tablespoon lemon juice
½ cup flour
A pinch of baking soda
½ cup water
3 and ½ tablespoon olive oil
Cooking spray

DIRECTIONS:

1.In a bowl, mix strawberries with half of sugar, sprinkle some flour, add lemon juice, whisk and pour into the baking dish that fits your air fryer and greased with cooking spray

2.In another bowl, mix flour with the rest of the sugar, baking powder and soda and stir well.

3.Add the olive oil and mix until the whole thing with your hands.

4.Add ½ cup water and spread over strawberries.

5.Introduce in the fryer at 355 0 F and bake for 25 minutes.

6.Leave cobbler aside to cool down, slice and serve.

Enjoy!

Nutrition: calories 221, fat 3, fiber 3, carbs 6, protein 9

Black Tea Cake

SERVING	PREP TIME	COOK TIME
12	15 MINS	25 MINS

INGREDIENTS:

6 tablespoons black tea powder
2 cups milk
½ cup butter
2 cups sugar
4 eggs
2 teaspoons vanilla extract
½ cup olive oil
3 and ½ cups flour
1 teaspoon baking soda
3 teaspoons baking powder
For the cream:
6 tablespoons honey
4 cups sugar
1 cup butter, soft

DIRECTIONS:

1.Put the milk in a pot, heat up over medium heat, add tea, stir well, take off heat and leave aside to cool down.

2.In a bowl, mix ½ cup butter with 2 cups sugar, eggs, vegetable oil, vanilla extract, baking powder, baking soda and 3 and ½ cups flour and stir everything really well.

3.Pour this into 2 greased round pans, introduce each in the fryer at 330 0 F and bake for 25 minutes.

4.In a bowl, mix 1 cup butter with honey and 4 cups sugar and stir really well.

5.Arrange one cake on a platter, spread the cream all over, top with the other cake and keep in the fridge until you serve it.

Enjoy it!

Nutrition: calories 200, fat 4, fiber 4, carbs 6, protein 2

Strawberry Shortcakes

SERVING	PREP TIME	COOK TIME
6	20 MINS	45 MINS

INGREDIENTS:

Cooking spray
¼ cup sugar+ 4 tablespoons
1 and ½ cup flour
1 teaspoon baking powder
¼ teaspoon baking soda
1/3 cup butter
1 cup buttermilk
1 egg, whisked
2 cups strawberries, sliced
1 tablespoon rum
1 tablespoon mint, chopped
1 teaspoon lime zest, grated
½ cup whipping cream

DIRECTIONS:

1.In a bowl, mix flour with ¼ cup sugar, baking powder and baking soda and stir.

2.In another bowl, mix buttermilk with egg, stir, add to flour mix and whisk.

3.Spoon this dough into 6 jars greased with cooking spray, cover with tin foil, arrange them in your air fryer cook at 360 0 F for 45 minutes.

4.Meanwhile, in a bowl, mix strawberries with 3 tablespoons sugar, rum, mint and lime zest, stir and leave aside in a cold place.

5.In another bowl, mix whipping cream with 1 tablespoon sugar and stir.

6.Take jars out, divide strawberry mix and whipped cream on top and serve.

Enjoy!

Nutrition: calories 164, fat 2, fiber 3, carbs 5, protein 2

SECTION TEN

Street Snacks

Sponge Cake

SERVING	PREP TIME	COOK TIME
12	10 MINS	20 MINS

INGREDIENTS:

3 cups flour
3 teaspoons baking powder
½ cup cornstarch
1 teaspoon baking soda
1 cup olive oil
1 and ½ cup milk
1 and 2/3 cup sugar
2 cups water
¼ cup lemon juice
2 teaspoons vanilla extract

DIRECTIONS:

1.Inside a bowl, mix flour with baking powder, baking soda,cornstarch and sugar and whisk well.

2.In another bowl, mix oil with milk, water, vanilla and lemon juice and whisk.

3.Combine the two mixtures, stir, pour in a greased baking dish that fits your air fryer, introduce in the fryer and cook at 350 0 F for 20 minutes.

4.Leave cake to cool down, cut and serve.

Enjoy!

Nutrition: calories 246, fat 3, fiber 1, carbs 6, protein 2

Ricotta and Lemon Cake

SERVING	PREP TIME	COOK TIME
4	10 MINS	1 HOUR + 10 MINS

INGREDIENTS:

8 eggs, whisked
3 pounds ricotta cheese
½ pound sugar
Zest from 1 lemon, grated
Zest from 1 orange, grated
Butter for the pan

DIRECTIONS:

1.In a bowl, mix eggs with sugar, cheese, lemon and orange zest and stir very well.

2.Grease a baking pan that fits your air fryer with some batter, spread ricotta mixture, introduce in the fryer at 390 0 F and bake for 30 minutes.

3.Reduce heat at 380 0 F and bake for 40 more minutes.

4.Take out of the oven, leave cake to cool down and serve!

Enjoy!

Nutrition: calories 110, fat 3, fiber 2, carbs 3, protein 4

Tangerine Cake

SERVING	PREP TIME	COOK TIME
8	10 MINS	20 MINS

INGREDIENTS:

¾ cup sugar
2 cups flour
¼ cup olive oil
½ cup milk
1 teaspoon cider vinegar
½ teaspoon vanilla extract
Juice and zest from 2 lemons
Juice and zest from 1 tangerine
Tangerine segments, for serving

DIRECTIONS:

1.In a bowl, mix flour with sugar and stir.

2.In another bowl, mix oil with milk, vinegar, vanilla extract, lemon juice and zest and tangerine zest and whisk very well.

3.Add flour, stir well, pour this into a cake pan that fits your air fryer, introduce in the fryer and cook at 360 0 F for 20 minutes.

4.Serve right away with tangerine segments on top.

Enjoy!

Nutrition: calories 180, fat 2, fiber 1, carbs 4, protein 4

Berries Mix

SERVING	PREP TIME	COOK TIME
4	5 MINS	6 MINS

INGREDIENTS:

2 tablespoons lemon juice
1 and ½ tablespoons maple syrup
1 and ½ tablespoons champagne vinegar
1 tablespoon olive oil
1 pound strawberries, halved
1 and ½ cups blueberries
¼ cup basil leaves, torn

DIRECTIONS:

1.In a pan that sizes your air fryer, mix lemon juice with maple syrup and vinegar, bring to a boil over medium high heat, add oil, blueberries and strawberries, stir, introduce in your air fryer and cook at 310 0 F for 6 minutes.

2.Sprinkle basil on top and serve!

Enjoy!

Nutrition: calories 163, fat 4, fiber 4, carbs 10, protein 2.1

Passion Fruit Pudding

SERVING	PREP TIME	COOK TIME
6	20 MINS	40 MINS

INGREDIENTS:

1 cup Paleo passion fruit curd
4 passion fruits, pulp and seeds
3 and ½ ounces maple syrup
3 eggs
2 ounces ghee, melted
3 and ½ ounces almond milk
½ cup almond flour
½ teaspoon baking powder

DIRECTIONS:

1.In a bowl, mix the half of the fruit curd with passion fruit seeds and pulp, stir and divide into 6 heat proof ramekins.

2.In a bowl, whisked eggs with maple syrup, ghee, the rest of the curd, baking powder, milk and flour and stir well.

3.Divide this into the ramekins as well, introduce in the fryer and cook at 200 0 F for 40 minutes.

4.Leave puddings to cool down and serve!

Enjoy!

Nutrition: calories 430, fat 22, fiber 3, carbs 7, protein 8

Air Fried Apples

SERVING	PREP TIME	COOK TIME
4	10 MINS	17 MINS

INGREDIENTS:

4 big apples, cored
A handful raisins
1 tablespoon cinnamon, ground
Raw honey to the taste

DIRECTIONS:

1.Fill each apple with raisins, sprinkle cinnamon, drizzle honey, put them in your air fryer and cook at 367 0 F for 17 minutes.

2.Leave them to cool down and serve.

Enjoy!

Nutrition: calories 220, fat 3, fiber 4, carbs 6, protein 10

Pumpkin Cookies

SERVING	PREP TIME	COOK TIME
24	10 MINS	15 MINS

INGREDIENTS:

2 and ½ cups flour
½ teaspoon baking soda
1 tablespoon flax seed, ground
3 tablespoons water
½ cup pumpkin flesh, mashed
¼ cup honey
2 tablespoons butter
1 teaspoon vanilla extract
½ cup dark chocolate chips

DIRECTIONS:

1.In a bowl, mix flax seed with water, stir and leave aside for a few minutes.

2.Mix flour with salt and baking soda in another bowl.

3.In a third bowl, mix honey with pumpkin puree, butter, vanilla extract and flaxseed.

4.Combine flour with honey mix and chocolate chips and stir.

5.Scoop 1 tablespoon of cookie dough on a lined baking sheet that fits your air fryer, repeat with the rest of the dough, introduce them in your air fryer and cook at 350 0 F for 15 minutes.

6.Leave cookies to cool down and serve.

Enjoy it!

Nutrition: calories 140, fat 2, fiber 2, carbs 7, protein 10

Tasty Orange Cookies

SERVING	PREP TIME	COOK TIME
8	10 MINS	12 MINS

INGREDIENTS:

2 cups flour
1 teaspoon baking powder
½ cup butter, soft
¾ cup sugar
1 egg, whisked
1 teaspoon vanilla extract
1 tablespoon orange zest, grated
For the filling:
4 ounces cream cheese, soft
½ cup butter
2 cups powdered sugar

DIRECTIONS:

1.In a bowl, mix cream cheese with ½ cup butter and 2 cups powdered sugar, stir well using your mixer and leave aside for now.

2.In another bowl, mix flour with baking powder.

3.In a third bowl, mix ½ cup butter with ¾ cup sugar, egg, vanilla extract and orange zest and whisk well.

4.Combine flour with orange mix, stir well and scoop 1 tablespoon of the mix on a lined baking sheet that fits your air fryer.

5.Repeat with the rest of the orange batter, introduce in the fryer and cook at 340 0 F for 12 minutes.

6.Leave cookies to cool down, spread cream filling on half of them top with the other cookies and serve.

Enjoy!

Nutrition: calories 124, fat 5, fiber 6, carbs 8, protein 4

SECTION ELEVEN

Brunch Recipes

Pineapple and Tofu Kabobs

Get ready for these simple and delicious kabobs with your wooden skewers.

INGREDIENTS:

1 block firm tofu
Cubed, 1 pineapple
Chopped into large chunks, 1 onion
chopped into large chunks, 1-2 bell peppers
Ingredients for Marinade
Tamari1/2 cup (or soy sauce or Braggs Liquid Aminos)
Water1/2 cup
maple syrup1/4 cup
1/2 tsp paprika
1/2 tsp ground ginger
Optional sriracha

DIRECTIONS:

To remove excess water, press the tofu. It's going to take about 10 minutes. Soak wooden skewers in water while the tofu is pressing. I broke mine in half to fit in with my Air Fryer.
In a shallow bowl or baking dish, mix the marinade.
Cube the tofu, then place the tofu for about 10 minutes in the marinade to soak.
Chop and set aside the veggies and pineapples.
Build the kabobs alternating on the skewers with vegetables, tofu, and pineapple.
While cooking for 15 minutes at 320 ° in Air Fryer, shake after 10 minutes. When cooking in a skillet, mix or turn tofu, pineapple, and veggies until lightly browned on all sides.
Use these ingredients and spices as a starting point, add to your favorites mushrooms, peppers, courgettes and more!
You should realize that cooking vegetables is quicker than tofu. If you use small pieces of veggies and large pieces of tofu, when you cook them for more than 15 minutesdry out.
One final tip! Cook your quinoa, rice or noodles with the remaining marinade! Use the leftover marinade in the skillet if you saute the veggies in a pan instead of making kabobs. These are some of the example pineapple, tofu, and veggies in a skillet. No oil was used to keep it from sticking, just the marinade or a little water.

Cheesy Potato Wedges

Consider these potato wedges if you love potato skins, but you want the potato as well. This is a great side dish and a friendly recipe for the game day!

INGREDIENTS:

Potatoes
1 pound fingerling potatoes
Extra-Virgin Olive Oil 1 Teaspoon (You Can Exclude This If You Don't' Eat Oil)
Kosher Salt1 Teaspoon
Ground Black Pepper1 Teaspoon
Garlic Powder1/2 Teaspoon
Cheese Sauce
Raw Cashews1/2 Cup
Ground Turmeric1/2 Teaspoon
Paprika1/2 Teaspoon
Nutritional Yeast2 Tablespoons
Fresh Lemon Juice1 Teaspoon
2 Tbsp To 1/4 Cup Water

DIRECTIONS:

Potatoes
Preheat the fryer for 3 minutes to 400 ° F. Wash the potatoes with it. Cut the potatoes and transfer them to a large bowl in half lengthwise. Add the potatoes with the oil (if used), salt, pepper and garlic powder. Toss to dress up. The potatoes are transferred to the air fryer. Cook, shaking halfway through the cooking time, for 16 minutes.

Cheese Sauce
Combine in a high-speed blender the cashews, turmeric, paprika, nutritional yeast, and lemon juice. Blend at low, increase speed gradually, and add water as required. Be careful not to use much water because you want the consistency to be thick and cheesy. Transfer the cooked potatoes or a piece of parchment paper to an air-fryer-safe pan. Drizzle the sauce over the wedges of the potato. Place the pan in the fryer and cook at 400 ° F for another 2 minutes.

Vegan Oil-free Tempura

It is necessary to batter the tempura dishes. Here are the cooking instructions and ingredients.

INGREDIENTS:

3 Tbsp flax meal
1/2 cup water
Place in the blender and mix for approximately 1 minute. The finished product will have a texture of the egg-white type allowing the dry coating to stick well. If you're planning to cook plenty of veggies, you're going to want to have plenty to double this.
Ingredients for dry coating:
1-1/2 cups panko bread crumbs
1 Tbsp onion powder
1 Tbsp garlic powder
3 Tbsp nutritional yeast
Place dry ingredients in a big bowl and whisk to mix well.

DIRECTIONS:

Slice the vegetables. The mushrooms I didn't cut, but I left them there. Drain and press the water before the tofu is sliced.
To make a wet coating, blend the flax and water. Place it in a pot.
Vegan Air Fryer Recipes batter for tempura
Flax and water, like white eggs, make a great consistency.
Roll each vegetable (or vegetable slice) in the wet batter to coat well.
Vegan Air Fryer Recipes cooking batter
This batter is dense and quickly sticks to the vegetables.
Next, dredge the chunks of vegetables in the dry cover.
Recipes for vegan air fryer. I like to use panko coating for crumbs of bread.
Put them in the air fryer basket and, if necessary, sprinkle with salt.
My air freyer is five quarters long and holds a lot.
Set the temperature at the following times to 400 degrees and timer.
20 minutes of asparagus, tofu, and broccoli.
Whole mushrooms, sweet potatoes, and onions from Jo Jo Jo—25 min.

NOTE: The only vegetable I precooked was the potatoes of Jo JoJo, just like the frites above.
Leave vegetables in the basket or put them on a plate once the air fryer timer is off and allow to cool. They're getting really brown and crispy.
See how they get crispy brown?
Serve and enjoy!

Air Fryer Jackfruit Taquitos

Such Vegan Air Fryer Jackfruit Taquitos have just four ingredients and take about half an hour to produce in the pressure cookeror on a stove, you can make the filling.

SERVING	PREP TIME	COOK TIME
2	10 MINS	20 MINS

INGREDIENTS:

1 1/4 ounce can water-packed jackfruit, rinsed and drained
1 cup canned or cooked red beans,drained and rinsed
4 6-inch corn or whole wheat tortillas
1/2 cup pico de gallo sauce
4 spritzes canola oil or extra-virgin olive oil
1/4 cup plus 2 tbsp water

DIRECTIONS:

Combine the jackfruit, rice, pico de gallo, and water in a medium saucepan or pressure cooker.
Heat the jackfruit mixture over medium - high heat until it starts to boil when you use a casserole. Reduce heat, cover the casserole and cook for 20 to 25 minutes.
Cover the pressure cooker, allow to cook for 3 minutes at low pressure, and then use a natural release.
Mash the mixture of jackfruits with a fork or potato masher. You're looking for a meaty texture to cut the jackfruit. For 3 minutes, preheat the air fryer to 370F.
Put a tortilla on the surface of the job. Spoon 1/4 cup of the mixture of jackfruit to the tortilla. Roll it tightly, pushing back into the tortilla any of the mixture that comes out. To make 4 taquitos, repeat this process.
Spritz the basket of the air fryer with the oil. Sprits also on the tops of the tortillas. Place the tortillas in the basket of the air fryer. Cook for eight minutes at 370F.

NOTE: The approximate time for cooking is based on the process of the pressure cooker, which is also the method I use in the video of the recipe.

Nutrition: Calories: 326kcal

Fish Taco
Crunch Wrap with Mango Salsa

YIELD: Four Crunchwraps
dairy and egg free, vegan

INGREDIENTS:

4 Large Burrito Size Tortillas
1 Small Yellow Onion, Peeled And Diced
A Small Red Bell Pepper, Seeded, Cored, And Diced
2 Cobs Fresh Grilled Corn, Cut From Cob
4 Pieces Fishless Filet
1/3 To 1/2 Cup Mango Salsa
Tortilla Chips (Ranch Bean And Rice Chips)
Mixed Greens (Romaine, Spinach, Radicchio)
4 Tablespoons Shredded Vegan Cheese

DIRECTIONS:

Preheat the oven to 400 ° F or prepare the fryer for the air.

Sprinkle the onion and bell pepper in the skillet over medium heat until soft, about five minutes. Add the grilled corn and sauté for a few more minutes.

Cook the Fishless Filets at 400 ° F for 6 minutes in the air fryer.

Cut into small pieces every cooked filet.

Crisp Wrap assembly: spoon a fourth of the pepper corn onion mixture into the tortilla middle. Add one Fishless Filet pieces, followed by two tablespoons of salsa.

Next, a few tortilla chips layer, then a big handful of mixed greens. Fold the sides of the tortilla to form a round wrap around the egg. Use a shredded cheese tablespoon as a' glue' to keep tortilla together, where all points are connected. Place the side of the cheese on the baking sheet for the oven or in the air fryer bowl. Repeat with the rest of the wraps.

In the oven: Cook the Crunchwrap for 9-10 minutes at 350°F.

In the air fryer: Cook the Crunchwrap for 6 minutes at 350°F.

Vegan BBQ Soy Curls

In a barbecue bowl with potato salad and collard greens, these vegan BBQ Soy Curls are fabulous. Cook them in a skillet or air fryer.

SERVING	PREP TIME	COOK TIME
2	13 MINS	8 MINS

INGREDIENTS:

1 cup warm water
1 teaspoon vegetarian Better Than Bouillon no chicken base
1 cup Soy Curls
1/4 cup BBQ sauce
1 teaspoon canola oil divided (Only if cooking in the skillet)

NOTE: You can also use a pinch of a bouillon cube instead of Best Than Bouillon or instead substitute the water with broth. Plain water is fine if you don't have any of the above.
When overcrowded in a skillet or air fryer, these BBQ Soy Curls get maximum crispiness & browning. So incase you want to double this recipe, depending on the size of your air fryer or skillet, you may need to cook in lots.

DIRECTIONS:

Soak soy curls for 10 minutes in water and bouillon in a mug. Drain in sieve soy coils, squeezing all the excess water.
Put the Soy Curls into a mixing bowl and turn the hydrated Soy Coils physically into shreds, like shredding string cheese.
TO COOK IN AN AIR FRYER: At 400 degrees, air fry the Soy Curls for 3 minutes. Remove Soy Curls from the air fryer, move them back to the mixing bowl and stir them in BBQ sauce. Make sure all the curls are coated uniformly. Switch to the fryer in the air. At 400 degrees, fry the air for 5 minutes, stopping twice to shake the pan.
TO COOK IN A SKILLET: Bring skillet with 1/2 teaspoon of oil to medium heat. Add the hydrated & squeezed Soy Curls to the pan and fry until they are dry and slightly crisp for 3 minutes. Remove Soy Curls from the skillet and return them to the mixing bowl. Toss them with a barbecue sauce to make sure that every Soy Curl is evenly coated. In skillet, put the remaining 1/2 teaspoon oil and cook Soy Curls for 4 minutes longer. Do not move too much of the Soy Curls in order to get some nice dark marks on them.
Serve the BBQ Soy Curls with vegan potato salad, collard greens and/or mac and cheese that is not dairy.

Nutrition: Calories: 136kcal | Carbohydrates: 18g | Protein: 7g | Fat: 3g | Sodium: 552mg | Potassium: 160mg | Fiber: 2g | Sugar: 12g | Vitamin A: 80IU | Calcium: 12mg | Iron: 2.4mg

Crispy Avocado Tacos

The ideal addition to your taco game is the panko-coated avocado fries. These tacos of Crispy Avocado are loaded with heavy corn and bean salad and creamy sriracha mayo.

SERVING	PREP TIME	COOK TIME
6	20 MINS	10 MINS

INGREDIENTS:

For the Corn and Bean Salad
can black beans1 15 ounce ,drained and rinsed
freshor frozen corn1 cup
1/4 cup chopped green onion
1 tsp garlic powder
1/2 tsp ground cumin
1/2 tsp coriander
1/2 tsp mild chipotle chile powder
Lime1 fresh – juiced
your favorite salsa1/4 cup – store or Homemade -bought is fine
For the Avocado Fries
Avocados2 Haas – pitted, peeled, and cut into 12 slices each (so 24 slices total)
Aquafaba3/4 cup – white bean or chickpea
panko breadcrumbs3/4 cup
1/2 tsp salt
For the Sriracha Mayo
vegan mayo3/4 cup
1 to 2 tbspsriracha sauce
For the Tacos
corn tortillas12 small – warmed

DIRECTIONS:

Preheat your oven to around400F, if you're planning to bake the avocado fries.
Make the Corn and Bean Salad
In a bowl, mix all the salad ingredients, then set aside. DO NOT cool down, particularly when using frozen corn. It will take time to thaw, which is why you first make the salad.
Make the Avocado Fries
Toss the panko and salt together in a shallow bowl. In another shallow bowl, dump the aquafaba.
Dredge the slices of avocado in the aquafaba and then get a good coating in the panko.
To Air Fry: Arrange the slices in your air fryer basket in a single layer. It is necessary to have a single layer. Please do not overlap! Air fry at 390F for 10 minutes (do not preheat) and after 5 minutes shake well. It may need to be performed in 2 batches.
To Bake: Arrange the slices on a flat sheet of baking. Ensure to bake on the middle rack of the oven for 20 minutes.
Have the Sriracha Mayo whisk together in a small bowl while the Avocado Fries Cook whisk the mayo ingredients.
Make Your Tacos
On each tortilla, spoon about 2 tablespoons of corn and bean salad, then add 2 slices of avocado on each. Spoon a generous sriracha mayo table spoon on top and serve.

NOTE: Serve as a spicy mayo finger food for dipping or stuffing it in sandwiches, tacos or burritos!

Nutrition: Calories: 400kcal

Air Fryer Sushi Roll

SERVING	PREP TIME	COOK TIME
3	1 HOUR + 10 MINS	10 MINS

INGREDIENTS:

For the Coating
For the Kale Salad Sushi Rolls
1 Batch Pressure Cooker Sushi Rice , Cooled To
Room Temperature
Panko Breadcrumbs 1/2 Cup
For Making Kale Salad
Chopped Kale With Ribs Removed 1 1/2 Cups
Rice Vinegar 1/2 Tspn
Toasted Sesame Oil 3/4 Tspn
Garlic Powder 1/8 Tspn
Ground Ginger 1/4 Tspn
Soy Sauce 3/4 Tspn
Make the Sriracha Mayo
vegan mayonnaise 1/4 cup
sriracha sauce, to taste
sesame seeds, toasted or not 1 tbsp
3 sheets of sushi nori
1/2 of a Haas avocado, sliced

DIRECTIONS:

Make the Kale Salad
Mix the kale, vinegar, sesame oil, garlic powder, soy sauce in a large bowl. Massage the kale with hands(ensure to clean hands properly) until it becomes bright green and wild. Remove the seeds of sesame and set aside.

Make the Kale Salad Sushi Rolls
Lay out a nori sheet on a dry surface. Grab a handful of rice with slightly damp fingertips and scatter it over the nori. The idea is to get a thin layer of rice that covers nearly the whole sheet. You're going to want to leave about 1/2" naked seaweed along one edge. Think of it as the flap that will shut down your roll.

Lay about 2-3 tablespoons of kale salad on the opposite end of the seaweed, and top with a few slices of avocado. Roll up your sushi from the end with the filling, pressing gently to get a nice, tight roll. Use that naked bit of seaweed make closed roll sealed when you get to the end. Get your fingertips wet if needed, and moist that bit of seaweed to make it stick properly. Repeat steps 2 and 3 in order to make 3 more sushi rolls.

Make the Sriracha Mayo
Whisk the vegan mayo together with sriracha in a shallow bowl until you hit the heat point you need. Start with 1 teaspoon and add 1/2 teaspoon at a time until you have your DREAMS ' spicy mayo!

Fry and Slice
In a shallow bowl, dump the panko breadcrumbs.
Take your first roll of sushi and cover it in the Sriracha Mayo as evenly as possible, then in the panko. Place the roll in your basket of air fryer. Repeat with the remaining rolls of your sushi. For 10 minutes, fry the air at 390F, shaking gently after about 5 minutes.

When the rolls are cool enough to handle, take a good knife and gently break the roll into 6-8 bits. Talk about slicing softly and when you're slicing don't press hard with your knife. That's just going to send out the ends of your roll of kale and avocado.

Serve with soy sauce for dipping.

Equipment

Air Fryer

Nutrition: Calories: 469kcal

Sweeet Potatos & Brussels Sprouts

Brussels sprouts this compact air fryer meal prep recipe stars, sweet potato, and two simple blender sauces to keep things interesting all week long!

SERVING	PREP TIME	COOK TIME
4	10 MINS	25 MINS

INGREDIENTS:

For the Veggies
6 cups diced sweet potato – You're going for 1" pieces.
spray oil
2 tspns garlic powder
Four cups of brussels sprouts–cut in 1/4 "thick bits lengthwise. Depending on the size of your Brussels, that could be fifth, third or quarter.
2 tbsp low-sodium soy sauce
For the Sweet Potato Meal Prep Containers
4 servings grain of your choice – See post above. I used quinoa in the video.
1 Batch 5-Minute Peanut Butter Sauce–if you prefer, you can do 1/2 batch, which will still be enough.
1 Magical Tahini Dressing batch–DO NOT halve this recipe–it's not going to mix well using less
1/4 cup green onion, chopped, optional

DIRECTIONS:

Make the Veggies
Add the sweet potatoes and spray them with oil to your air fryer, shaking to brush. Sprinkle with the garlic powder on 1 teaspoon and shake again. Cook for 15 minutes at 400F, shaking 8 minutes later.
Add the sprouts from Brussels to the basket, spray with oil again, and sprinkle with more garlic powder. Shake well, then cook at 400F for 5 minutes.
Sprinkle on the soy sauce, shake to cover the vegetables, open the air fryer. Set the air fryer to cook for about 5 minutes, but check in for 2 minutes and 3 minutes each time you shake. Cooking times can be different! When browned and soft, the veggies are done.
Assemble The Sweet Potato Meal Prep Containers Combine 4 meal prep containers and split between them the grains and the veggie mix.
Attach 2-3 tablespoons of peanut sauce and attach 2-3 tablespoons of tahini dressing to each of the other two. Sprinkle over each meal with a tablespoon of chopped green onion.
Storage: 4 days in the fridge.
Equipment

Air Fryer

NOTE: Calorie estimates used quinoa as a grain and 2 spoons per tub of sauce. Sprinkle the nuts or seeds to the mix if you want to make this even more satisfying. When I'm really hungry, I like to add roasted cashews or pumpkin seeds to myself.

Nutrition: Calories: 469kcal

SECTION TWELVE

Desserts

and Sweets Recipes

Quick Air Fryer Apple Pie

I used "unique" pie plates with a 5-inch oven-safe. Any oven-safe pan or dish is going to do it, just make sure it fits with a little space on all sides in your air fryer tub.

SERVING	COURSE	COOKING METHOD
4	DESSERT	AIR FRYER

INGREDIENTS:

3 apples peeled, cored and then diced
1 tablespoon lemon juice
1/8 cup sugar
1 teaspoon ground cinnamon
Salt a pinch
1 1/2 tablespoons all-purpose flour
Sugar for dusting
1 9-inch prepared vegan piecrust dough

DIRECTIONS:

In a cup, mix apples, juice of lemon, sugar, cinnamon, salt and flour. Set it aside.
Split the pie in half. Set aside half of it.
Preheat the fryer for 5 minutes at 400 ° F.
Split the half-pie crust into two pieces. Roll out in a round for half. Mold it on the bottom of a pan / dish of5-inch pie, bringing the side up to halfway.
 Put 1/3 of the mixture of apples into the dough. Roll the other half of the dough into a round and pinch the dough down over the apples to reach the lower half of the dough on the ground. Cut the top of the steam vents. Sprinkle with water and sugar.
If you've got a second pie / dish of 5 inches, repeat.
Put a pie pan* in the air fryer preheated. Cook 4 minutes at 400 ° F.
Lower heat to 330 ° F, and cook in the airfryer for 20 minutes longer.

Recipe Notes: You may be able to cook two small pies at once, depending on the size of the air fryer, and if you have a rack adapter.

Whether you make two 5-inch pies, the apple mixture leftover will be about 1/3. Freeze. Freeze. Thaw it later, mix it with 1/2 cup uncooked rolled oats and cook in a ramekin or small cast iron crock at 350 ° F for 12 minutes.

Small Batch Brownies

Everyone enjoys brownies, and we love them a little too much in our room. I started making small batches with that said that we can't get into trouble eating too many. It's a bonus that the air fry doesn't heat up your entire house like an oven, and baking for summer dinner parties is a perfect treat.

SERVING	PREP TIME	COOK TIME
4	10 MINS	20 MINS

DRY INGREDIENTS:

1/2 cup whole wheat pastry flour , (*use gluten-free baking blend)
1/2 cup vegan sugar , (or sweetener of choice, to taste)
1/4 cup cocoa powder
1 tablespoon ground flax seeds
1/4 teaspoon salt

WET INGREDIENTS:

1/4 cup non-dairy milk
1/4 cup aquafaba
1/2 teaspoon vanilla extract
MIX-INS
1/4 cup of any one or a combination of the following: chopped walnuts, hazelnuts, pecans, mini vegan chocolate chips, shredded coconut

DIRECTIONS:

For one pot, add the dry ingredients. Then combine in a large measuring cup the wet ingredients. Apply the wet and blend well to the dry.
Add and mix in the mix-in(s) of your choosing.
Preheat your air fryer to 350 degrees (or as close as it comes to your air fryer). To keep it fully oil-free, just spray some oil on a 5-inch cake or pie round pan (or a loaf pan that works in your air fryer).
Put the pan in the basket for the fryer. Cook twenty minutes. If the middle is not well positioned or when stuck in the middle cook for 5 minutes more, a knife does not come out clean and repeat as needed. Depending on the size of the pan and your particular air fryer, the time may vary.

Nutrition: Calories: 225.3kcal | Carbohydrates: 41g | Protein: 4g | Fat: 6.8g | Sodium: 157.8mg | Potassium: 169mg | Fiber: 4.8g | Sugar: 25g | Vitamin A: 30IU | Calcium: 35mg | Iron: 1.5mg

Air fryer Strawberry Cupcakes

Welcome with fluffy strawberry frosting to my Air Fryer strawberry cupcakes. I absolutely hated the first time I had a cupcake and I couldn't even finish it.

SERVING	PREP TIME	COOK TIME
10	15 MINS	8 MINS

INGREDIENTS:

100 g Butter
100 g Caster Sugar
2 Medium Eggs
100 g Self Raising Flour
½ Tsp Vanilla Essence
50 g Butter
100 g Icing Sugar
½ Tsp Pink Food Colouring
1 Tbsp Whipped Cream
¼ Cup Fresh Strawberries blended

DIRECTIONS:

Preheat the airfryer to 170c.
While it is heating up, cream the butter and sugar in a large mixing bowl. Do this until the mixture is light and fluffy.
Add the vanilla essence and beat in the eggs one at a time. After adding each egg add a little of the flour. Gently fold in the rest of the flour.
Add them to little bun cases so that they are 80% full. Place them in the airfryer and then cook for 8 minutes on 170c.
While the cupcakes are cooking make the topping. Cream the butter and gradually add the icing sugar until you have a creamy mixture. Add the food colouring, whipped cream and blended strawberries and mix well.
Once the cupcakes are cooked, using a piping bag add your topping to them doing circular motions so that you have that lovely cupcake look.

Serve!

Recipe Notes:
I prefer fresh strawberries in my cupcake frosting. But if you prefer frozen you can use those if you wish. If you do increase the measurements by a third as they are not as strong flavoured as fresh.

Nutrition:
Calories: 236kcal | Carbohydrates: 27g | Protein: 2g | Fat: 13g | Saturated Fat: 8g | Cholesterol: 65mg | Sodium: 120mg | Potassium: 27mg | Fiber: 0g | Sugar: 20g | Vitamin A: 420IU | Vitamin C: 2.1mg | Calcium: 10mg | Iron: 0.3mg

Air Fryer Lemon Butterfly Buns

Welcome to my butterfly buns with cherries on top of my Air fryer lemon. I'm missing the British bakery living in Portugal.

SERVING	PREP TIME	COOK TIME
12	15 MINS	8 MINS

INGREDIENTS:

100 g Butter
100 g Caster Sugar
2 Medium Eggs
100 g Self Raising Flour
½ Tsp Vanilla Essence
1 Tsp Cherries
50 g Butter
100 g Icing Sugar
½ Small Lemon juice and rind
Metric - Imperial

DIRECTIONS:

Preheat to 170c the airfryer.
Cream the butter with the sugar in a large mixing bowl until light and smooth.
Add the essence of vanilla.
Beat the eggs (one at a time) to make sure you add each one a little flour.
Fold gently into the rest of the flour.
Before you run out of cases, fill the mixture with half of the small bun cases. Place the first six (I can fit just six in mine) in your Airfryer and cook for eight minutes on 170c.
Prepare the icing sugar while the buns are frying–cream the butter and gradually add it to the icing sugar. Place the lemon together and blend well. put a little water if it's too thick.
Once the butterfly buns have finished cooking, remove the top slice from the buns and slice in half, turning them into butterfly shapes. Place the icing sugar in the middle to keep it in place. Layer on top 1/3 of a cherry and sieve with some icing sugar.

Serve!

Notes: The fair proportions are what I love about this pot. Remembering how much you need to weigh is always challenging. But it makes it easy to adjust with the same amounts of butter, sugar and flour if you need to make a larger or smaller one.

Nutrition: Calories: 196kcal | Carbohydrates: 23g | Protein: 2g | Fat: 10g | Saturated Fat: 6g | Cholesterol: 54mg | Sodium: 100mg | Potassium: 24mg | Fiber: 0g | Sugar: 16g | Vitamin A: 350IU | Vitamin C: 2.4mg | Calcium: 10mg | Iron: 0.2mg

Flourless Key Lime Cupcakes

SERVING	PREP TIME	COOK TIME
6	10 MINS	20 MINS

INGREDIENTS:

250 g Greek Yoghurt
200 g Soft Cheese
2 Large Eggs
1 Large Egg yolk only
¼ Cup Caster Sugar
1 Tsp Vanilla Essence
2 Limes juice and rind
Metric - Imperial

DIRECTIONS:

Mix the Greek yogurt and the soft cheese with a wooden spoon or a hand mixer until they are smooth and fluffy and like a mayonnaise.
Add the eggs, then mix. Remove and blend the sugar, vanilla essence and limes.
Now you're going to have a wonderful creamy combine and you're going to have to fill 6 cases with the contents. Put the rest later on to one side.
Bake the cupcakes in the Airfryer at 160c for 10 minutes and then at 180c for a further 10 minutes.
While the cupcakes are cooking remove the contents of your bowl into a cupcake nozzle and place in the fridge for 10 minutes.
Once the cupcakes are baked, they will cool down on a baking tray for 10 minutes. EOLBREAK Create your cupcakes ' top layer when the nozzle is cold. Place your cupcake topping properly and decorate it with spare limes for 4 hours fridge.

Recipe Notes: For the first batch, I used a hand mixer, but when I tried the second time, I found it easier with a wooden spoon.

Nutrition: Calories: 218kcal | Carbohydrates: 13g | Protein: 9g | Fat: 14g | Saturated Fat: 7g | Cholesterol: 120mg | Sodium: 155mg | Potassium: 99mg | Fiber: 0g | Sugar: 11g | Vitamin A: 600IU | Vitamin C: 6.5mg | Calcium: 101mg | Iron: 0.6mg

Air Fryer
Fruit Crumble Mug Cakes

SERVING	PREP TIME	COOK TIME
4	15 MINS	15 MINS

INGREDIENTS:

110 g Plain Flour
50 g Butter
30 g Caster Sugar
30 g Gluten Free Oats
25 g Brown Sugar
4 Plums
1 Small Apple
1 Small Pear
1 Small Peach
Handful Blueberries
1 Tbsp Honey
Metric - Imperial

DIRECTIONS:

Preheat the Air Fryer to 160c.
Using the corer detach from the fruit the cores and stones and dice into very small pieces of square.
Put the fruit between the four mugs in the bottom of the mugs. Sprinkle with brown sugar and honey until well covered with all the fruit. Put side by side.
In a mixing bowl, put the flour, butter and caster sugar and rub the fat in the flour. You can then apply the oats when it looks like fine breadcrumbs. Play well with each other.
Cover the tops of the mugs with a layer of your crumble.
Place at 160c for 10 minutes in the Air Fryer. Then cook at 200c for another 5 minutes after 10 minutes so you can get a nice crunch to the top of the crumble.

Notes: We used gluten-free oats as the flour could be pretty heavy and this really balanced it out. For whatever fruit you have, you can also change it a little, because we think rhubarb works really well too.

Nutrition: Calories: 380kcal | Carbohydrates: 68g | Protein: 5g | Fat: 11g | Saturated Fat: 6g | Cholesterol: 26mg | Sodium: 93mg | Potassium: 331mg | Fiber: 5g | Sugar: 36g | Vitamin A: 685IU | Vitamin C: 12.8mg | Calcium: 27mg | Iron: 1.9mg

Delicious British Lemon Tarts

SERVING	PREP TIME	COOK TIME
8 TARTS	15 MINS	15 MINS

INGREDIENTS:

100 g Butter
225 g Plain Flour
30 g Caster Sugar
1 Large Lemon zest and juice
4 TspMrs Darlington's Lemon Curd
Pinch Nutmeg
Metric – Imperial

DIRECTIONS:

Make your shortcrust pastry in a large mixing bowl. Blend butter, flour and sugar together using the process of rubbing. Add the lemon rind and juice, nutmeg, then blend again when it looks like fine breadcrumbs. Use the water to combine the ingredients to add water a little while until you have lovely soft dough.

Roll out your pastry with a little flour.

Rub a little flour around them using small ramekins or small pastry cases to avoid them from sticking and then apply your pastry. Please ensure that your pastry is nice and thin otherwise it will end up too thick when baked.

In each of your mini tart pots, add 1/2 teaspoon and cook your lemon tarts on 180c for 15 minutes.

Leave to cool for a couple of minutes and then serve.

Notes: I was told by the people behind the lemon curd not to cook it and then eat it because it's already baked, but I noticed that it cooked perfectly as long as you didn't take the temperature above 180c. But if I cook it and keep the heat to a limit, I wouldn't mix it with other stuff.
After cooking the pastry, before you add the lemon curd, cook the pastry for 10 minutes, then add the lemon curd. Put them in the fridge for 20 minutes after that.

Nutrition: Protein: 3g | Fat: 10g | Sodium: 100mg | Saturated Fat: 6g | Carbohydrates: 27g | Cholesterol: 26mg | Potassium: 30mg |Calories: 218kcal | Fiber: 0g | Sugar: 5g | Vitamin A: 310IU | Vitamin C: 1mg | Calcium: 7mg | Iron: 1.3mg

Air Fryer Pumpkin Pie

Pumpkin Pie Air Fryer. Two easy ways in the air fryer to make pumpkin pie. Our home-made pumpkin pie air fryer version is delicious and includes homemade pumpkin pie crust. Great for either the fryer air or the oven fryer air.

SERVING	PREP TIME	COOK TIME
8	10 MINS	29 MINS

INGREDIENTS:

Kitchen Gadgets:
Air Fryer
Instant Pot
Pie Pan
Sieve

Air Fryer Pie Crust Ingredients:
225 g Plain Flour
100 g Butter
25 g Caster Sugar
1 Tbsp Cinnamon
1 Tsp Nutmeg

Air Fryer Pumpkin Pie Filling:
450 g Pumpkin
3 Cm Ginger
3 Large Eggs
250 g Brown Sugar
60 ml Whole Milk
240 ml Double Cream
3 Tbsp Corn Flour
2 Tbsp Cinnamon
1 Tsp Nutmeg
Metric – Imperial

DIRECTIONS:

Make your seasoned pie crust. In a bowl mix your diced butter into your flour until it resembles coarse breadcrumbs. Add in the sugar, cinnamon and nutmeg. Mix well adding a little water at a time until you have a dry pie crust. Roll out your pie crust and place it in your pie pan.

Cook Your Pumpkin. Add your cubed pumpkin and cubed ginger into the Instant Pot and add 1 cup of water. Set to manual pressure/pressure cook for 4 minutes. Use quick pressure release and manually release pressure.

Drain Your Instant Pot. Using a sieve remove the liquid from your Instant Pot and then drain using a milk cloth. This will remove any excess liquid as pumpkin carries a lot and if you don't it can stop your pumpkin pie from setting.

Make your pumpkin pie filling. Place your drained pumpkin and ginger back in the Instant Pot and add all the pumpkin filling ingredients apart from the cream. Mix the eggs and other ingredients in the pumpkin with a hand mixer until you have a smooth, thin pumpkin sauce.. Whisk in the double cream and mix well.

Place the pumpkin pie filling into the pie crust making sure it doesn't go more than 1cm off the top. As otherwise it will be hard to handle and likely to leak over the top.

Cook the pumpkin pie in the air fryer. Place the pumpkin pie on the middle shelf and cook for 25 minutes at 180c/360f.

Move to the fridge and allow to cool overnight. This will help firm up your pumpkin pie and then the next day it will be ready for slicing.

NOTE: The method above is based upon a full pumpkin pie in the air fryer oven. To adjust for pumpkin pie tarts, keep the same cook time and roll out into mini pie cases.

The only difference is you make a mini version for a smaller air fryer. You don't need to blind bake your pie crust. If you blind bake you end up with overcooked pie crust. The flavour of the pumpkin pie is so much nicer with fresh ginger.

If you want to quickly work out size imagine the length of your thumb and then chop it into small bite sized chunks. The nutritional information is based on each slice if you cut it into 8 once cooked.

Nutrition: Calories: 491kcal | Carbohydrates: 66g | Protein: 7g | Fat: 24g | Saturated Fat: 14g | Cholesterol: 130mg | Sodium: 138mg | Potassium: 326mg | Fiber: 3g | Sugar: 36g | Vitamin A: 5643IU | Vitamin C: 5mg | Calcium: 111mg | Iron: 3mg

Pumpkin Pancakes

INGREDIENTS:

1 large pumpkin (shredded)
1 ½ cups almond flour
3 eggs
2 tsp. dried basil
2 tsp. dried parsley
Salt and Pepper to taste
3 tbsp. Butter

DIRECTIONS:

Preheat to 250 Fahrenheit the air fryer.
In a small bowl, add the ingredients together. Ensure a mixture that is smooth and well balanced.
Take a mold for a pancake and add butter to it. Add the batter to the mold and put it in the air fryer basket.
Cook until browned on both sides of the pancake and serve with maple syrup.

Oats Muffins

INGREDIENTS:

2 cups All-purpose flour
Milk 1 ½ cup
Baking powder ½ tsp.
Baking soda ½ tsp.
Butter 2 tbsp.
Sugar 1 cup
Vinegar 3 tsp.
Oats 1 cup
Vanilla essence ½ tsp.
Muffin cups or butter paper cups.

DIRECTIONS:

Mix the ingredients together and add acrumbly with your fingers.
The milk would have to be split into two parts and add one part to the baking soda and the other part to the vinegar. Now, blend together the two milk mixtures and wait before the milk begins foaming. Add this to the crumbly mixture and start very quickly whisking the ingredients. You'll need to transfer the mixture into a muffin cup and set aside once you've got a smooth batter.
For five minutes, preheat the fryer to 300 Fahrenheit. The muffin cups will need to be put in the basket and sealed. Cook the muffins for 15 minutes and test whether or not a toothpick is used to cook the muffins. Remove and serve hot cups.

Do not go yet; One last thing to do...

If you enjoyed this book or found it useful I'd be very grateful if you'd post a short review on **Amazon**. Your support really does make a difference and I read all the reviews personally so I can get your feedback and make this book even better.

Thanks again for your support!

CPSIA information can be obtained
at www.ICGtesting.com
Printed in the USA
LVHW100806230221
679512LV00006B/100